Table of Contents

Working with Wood

WORKING WITH
WOOD

Landauer Books

Working with WOOD

32 Essential Skills for Building Cabinets & Furniture

Distributed by Landauer Corporation
3100 NW 101st Street, Suite A
Urbandale, Iowa 50322
800-557-2144; www.landauercorp.com

CREDITS

Tom Carpenter
Creative Director

Mark Johanson
Book Products Development Manager
Handyman Club of America

Dan Cary
Photo Production Coordinator

Chris Marshall
Editorial Coordinator

Bill Nelson
Series Design, Art Direction and Production

Mark Macemon
Lead Photographer

Kim Bailey
Photography

Tom Deveney
Robert Ginn
Technical Advisors and Builders

Landauer ISBN 13: 978-1-890621-95-7
Landauer ISBN 10:   1-890621-95-1

10 9 8 7 6 5 4 3 2 1
Printed in USA

Introduction

The tree grows. It's felled and sawn into pieces of lumber. The lumber is kiln-dried, or the woodcutter may leave it to dry in an open-air shed. A creative mind sees in the lumber stack a piece of furniture, household objects, a boat, crafts. The woodworker builds them. The non-woodworker marvels at the results that come from the shop.

Yet all that separates a woodworker from a would-be woodworker is practice, experience and desire.

If you want to be a woodworker, the good news is there is no mystery to it; all you really need is some dexterity and patience. Woodworking simply is the manipulation of wood using a set of readily acquired tools and easily learned skills.

Building woodworking projects requires you to solve a myriad of design and construction problems. As you learn and as you build, you'll have to make many decisions: What do I want to build? How big should it be? What do I want it to look like? What type of wood should I use? What hardware and tools do I need to build it? How do I join the pieces together? Does it need doors or drawers? How will I finish it?

This book provides you with the knowledge you'll need to ask the right questions, answer them, make decisions appropriate to the projects you want to build. The most fun way to accumulate this information is to construct projects that you'll enjoy building and using. The projects in this book provide the experience you need.

The focus of this book is on building cabinets and furniture, both for indoors and outdoors. The difference between cabinets and furniture is basic: Cabinets are primarily boxes designed for storage that can be built-in or moveable—such as kitchen cabinets, medicine chests, bookcases and wall units. Furniture, on the other hand, is moveable, like tables and chairs. The projects are presented more or less in order of difficulty, from simplest to most complicated. New techniques and information are introduced in each successive project.

You'll learn about the types of woods available at lumberyards and home centers:
• Which types of wood are easy to cut and shape.
• Which types require more patience and skill to plane and smooth.
• Which woods accept which stains and finishes best.

You'll also learn how to make a variety of joints, from the dado to the dovetail, and when each joint is appropriate to use.

All of the project chapters in this book include the information you need to construct the projects exactly as shown. However, you should feel free to redesign any of these projects to suit your own needs. The bookcase in chapter one may be too big or small for your room. You may want the garden bench shown in chapter six to comfortably seat three people, instead of two, as it was designed to do. You might prefer to use less expensive pine to build the Shaker table, which we construct from maple in chapter two. If cutting dovetails to build the cherry hope chest in chapter seven would be too time-consuming, you can opt to use biscuit joints.

By the time you've learned all the skills shown in this book, you'll not only be able to modify these projects, but you'll also be well on the road to designing and building your dream projects.

Learning woodworking is a lifelong pursuit. It takes many years of patience to acquire the skills that come only from practice and experience. But the fundamentals are here. Even intermediate and experienced woodworkers will learn new techniques, for no two woodworkers' experiences are exactly the same. In time you'll develop your own style and techniques and pass them on to other woodworkers.

IMPORTANT NOTICE

Careful measuring and marking of project parts is of critical importance to any woodworking project, from the simplest to the most advanced.

And include sketches of the major joints. These are usually larger, often full-scale, drawings.

Use your drawing to create a list of workpieces, including dimensions, that's similar to the cutting lists that accompany the projects in this book. The cutting list, in turn, is the basis for your shopping list to bring to the lumberyard.

Woodworking Basics

Each woodworking project has its own unique set of challenges, from design to finish. But there are many general ways of working and a good deal of fundamental information common to any woodworking project you build.

Planning

Before you build any project, visualize how you want it to look and how you plan to build it, then translate your vision onto paper in the form of a drawing. This is your blueprint, which of course you can modify as you work (and more often than not, you will modify it). You don't have to be an artist to create workable shop drawings. A scaled drawing on graph paper may be helpful for working out scrolled patterns or shaped edges. But all that's usually needed is a simple sketch showing a front view and, in some cases, a side view. Be sure to include overall project dimensions on the sketch, as well.

Selecting & buying wood

Selecting a wood species and making your wood purchase are key starting points in any project. Throughout this book you'll find information on the types of wood we used for each project. These will help you in making some basic determinations about what type of wood is best suited for your project.

Hardwood is normally sold by the board foot (See photos, above). A board foot is the equivalent of a board that's 1 in. thick × 12 in. wide × 12 in. long. You can calculate the number of board feet in any piece of lumber by multiplying the three dimensions of the board (thickness, width and length), then dividing that number by 144 if all the dimensions are expressed in inches. If one of the dimensions is expressed in feet, divide by 12.

Common wood defects

Bowing

Crooking

Cupping

Twisting

For example, a 2-in. × 6-in. × 48-in. board has 4 board feet (2 times 6 times 48, divided by 144). Calculate the number of board feet you'll need for your projects and buy between 10 and 25 percent more than you need. There's always waste, either because of wood defects or because you simply can't use solid wood with 100 percent efficiency.

With the exception of pine, most woods you buy will be rough on one or more surfaces. It's sold in nominal dimensions such as 4/4, 5/4, 6/4 and so forth. An unsurfaced piece of 4/4 lumber is actually 1 in. thick. But after both sides are surfaced and ready to use—either at the mill or in your shop with your thickness planer—the actual thickness will be about 7/8 in. Most of the projects in this book call for 7/8-in. stock for this reason. To get a full inch out of the stock, you'd need to purchase 5/4 or 6/4 wood, only to end up with quite a bit of waste (not to mention a lot of time at the thickness planer).

When purchasing your lumber, its almost always worth the time to hand-select the boards. In addition to searching for the boards with the most pleasing color and grain, there are a number of wood defects to be on the lookout for. For example: warping, bowing, spalling, checking, cupping, crooking, and twisting. Also check the boards to make sure you've got enough clear (knot-free) lumber to cut your parts. If you do a little scouting around, you can sometimes save money by buying lower grade lumber and cutting around the wood defects.

Spalling is a gray to green permanent discoloration of the wood caused by fungal growth.

Knots should be avoided when purchasing hardwoods, but in some cases you may be able to work around them.

Checking is a splitting of the wood grain at the end of the board. It can be cut off, but it may indicate that the board was not cured properly, and is better avoided.

1 Run the board or boards through your surface planer to create at least one smooth face.

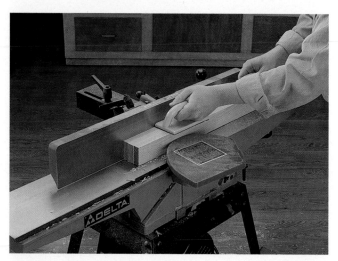

2 Joint one edge of the board (or glued-up stock) on your jointer until it's perfectly flat and smooth.

3 Rip-cut the board or panel to width on your table saw, making sure the jointed edge is riding against the fence.

Squaring your workpieces

Most of the wood project parts you'll work with must have square ends and edges. To be square means each face of a workpiece is at a right angle to the adjacent faces. Check edges for square before and after you cut workpieces to size. When you work with rough lumber, the first step in obtaining square is to plane smooth one face on a thickness planer, then plane one edge on a jointer. If the jointer fence is square to the jointer table, you'll end up with a square edge. Always use a try square to measure the edges of workpieces. You can also square edges on a table saw (if the saw blade is square to the table), with a router and straight bit guided by a straightedge or, with practice, with a hand-held smoothing or jointing plane.

Surfaced lumber generally comes with square edges. Still, check it with your try square.

You can square the ends of boards by crosscutting workpieces on a table saw (if the miter gauge is square to the blade) or a radial arm saw (if the fence is square to the blade). Check ends for square with a try square or, for larger pieces, with a carpenter's square.

When working with plywood, the edges and ends milled at the plywood plant can usually be relied on to be square. In fact, if you're searching for a straight-edge to use as a tool guide, for example to guide the router as described above, plywood's factory edge is as reliable as any. When ripping or crosscutting plywood, therefore, it's a good idea to mark the factory edges as you work.

Squaring your projects

Once your workpieces are square, you've made an important step toward constructing perfectly square projects: that is, projects that rest squarely on the floor, allow doors and drawers to close properly, and won't fail over time because of stresses at work on project joints and parts. Even with square workpieces, you need to monitor the squareness of a project as you assemble it.

Workpieces designed to be the same length as one another must, in fact, be the exact same length. A four-sided bookcase with unequal sides will end up not as a square or rectangle, but as an irregular (and unstable) quadrangle.

All parts must be the proper length. When you glue a partition into a bookcase, for example, the shelves above and below the partition will be concave if the partition is shorter than the opening, or convex if the partition is too long.

A glued-up project must be a square unit, not a parallelogram. Check your project for square as soon as you've glued and clamped it together. The best way to do this is to measure the diagonals for square with a tape measure (See photo, right). Measure a diagonal from one inside corner to the opposite inside corner, then measure the other diagonal in the same fashion. The diagonals should be equal. If not, you can force the cabinet square by pushing the opposite corners of the longer diagonal together until the diagonals are equal (this may require a helper). Measure the diagonals after each effort until you get it right.

Sometimes the pressure of the clamps won't allow you to force the project into square. In this case, simply loosen the clamps a bit and try again.

A third option is to use the pressure exerted by the clamps to square the cabinet. Normally, clamps should be parallel to the members being glued. But by orienting the clamps at a slight angle to those members, you can manipulate the clamping forces to work for you. In practice, you want to move the clamp jaw on the shorter diagonal away from the member, which lengthens the diagonal when the clamp is retightened.

Dry-assembling

No matter the project, the last step before assembling a project with glue is to assemble it without glue. A dry assembly lets you test how individual joints go together and how all the parts fit as a whole. If necessary, use clamps and the same wood blocks, cauls, or other clamp fittings you'll use for the real glue-up. Making adjustments as needed—paring a tenon or dovetail slightly—before applying glue ensures that the project will go together as you intended.

Preparing for glue-up

With pieces cut to size, marked ("left side, right side, top," etc.) and ready to be joined, you're ready for the most exciting and potentially harrowing woodworking experience of all—gluing-up. To ensure all the work you've put in beforehand comes to fruition, you must approach the glue-up session methodically, and you must work quickly, for once you apply glue to the two parts of a joint, capillary action begins to work. Wood pores absorb the

Measure the distance between opposite corners of a carcase (or any part you want to check for square). If measuring the diagonals (as this process is known) yields equal numbers, then the project is in square. If not, adjust the clamping pressure and corner angles until the diagonals are the same.

Selecting the correct glue and having it close at hand, along with glue applicators, is mostly a matter of preparation. Before beginning the glue-up, make sure the nozzles or tips on the glue bottles are clear and that the glue itself is not dried out or overly thickened. And make sure you've got enough on hand for the entire project.

Wood caul

The glue-up represents the moment of truth to woodworkers. Make sure you're prepared by having all materials well labeled and getting an extra hand or two if needed. Have a strategy in mind for making the assembly before you start. Make sure to have plenty of clamps and wood cauls on hand.

The point of joints

Much of woodworking boils down to one essential process: making joints. Joints were developed to counteract the forces of wood itself, which continues to move long after a tree is cut down. Wood movement occurs when wood absorbs moisture, causing wood fibers to swell, or when it desorbs moisture, causing shrinkage. Glue alone is no guarantee that two pieces of wood will stay bonded together as they expand and contract or undergo the stresses of normal wear and tear.

By cutting a joint, you increase the gluing surface and therefore create a stronger bond. Moreover, a properly designed joint exposes more long grain, and long-grain-to-long-grain joints are the most desirable. If you try to glue two pieces together end-grain-to-end-grain, you'll have a time of it.

Joints not only increase the gluing surface, but also provide a mechanical bond between two pieces of wood. Properly designed joints also allow wood to move while the joint remains strong.

glue's moisture, expanding the wood and making it difficult at best to fit joints together. (For example, unless you work quickly, the tongue that fit into the groove so perfectly during your dry-assembly run will swell and will no longer fit.)

To work quickly, you need to be thoroughly prepared. Preparation begins with having the appropriate tools and materials nearby, namely:

• A plastic squeeze bottle (filled with glue) with an applicator.

• A small bucket of clean water.

• A clean sponge.

• Glue applicators—a glue brush or a stick of wood that's about $\frac{1}{8} \times \frac{1}{4} \times 3$ in. in size.

• Wooden clamp blocks (cauls) lined with masking tape. The blocks can be hardwood or plywood, and you should have a variety of sizes on hand; assembly instructions in each chapter specify the best type of glue block for each project. The masking tape prevents the cauls from being glued to the workpieces. If the tape sticks to a workpiece, it can be scraped off with a cabinet scraper.

• Clamps—how many and of what variety is determined by the project.

Here are a few more tips to bear in mind before you begin a glue-up session:

• Lay out a specific glue-up area. The area should be large enough for the workpieces to be laid out or otherwise organized in a logical glue-up sequence.

How to plug screw counterbores

1 Use a counterbore bit to counterbore the pilot hole for the screw (⅜ in. is the standard counterbore diameter).

2 Apply glue to the end of a wood plug and insert it into the counterbore hole. You can buy plugs or make your own with a plug cutter.

3 Trim and sand the plug until it's even with the surrounding wood surface, then finish-sand the project.

• Lay out your workpieces in a logical glue-up sequence. That may mean laying two cabinet sides dado-side up, edges aligned, with the top, the bottom and the fixed shelves stacked or lined up in order.

• Determine whether your work table is large enough for the project, or whether you need to work on sawhorses or on the floor.

• You may need to line the worksurface with wax

TIP: Home-made oil finish

For a lustrous, protective finish that's perfect for rich woods like walnut, mix equal parts boiled linseed oil, turpentine and varnish. Apply the finish in two or three thin coats.

paper or newspaper to catch glue squeeze-out.

• Have several wood blocks handy to raise a partially glued project off the work surface in the event you need to slide in clamps or wood cauls to complete the glue-up effort.

Gluing & clamping

When you finally do glue up a project, apply just enough glue to cover the entire joint surface area, but not so much that you get excessive glue squeeze-out. Apply moderate clamping pressure— beginning woodworkers tend to overtighten clamps, believing that extra pressure will create a better joint. In fact, overtightening can squeeze too much glue from the joint and starve the joint of glue. One final note about developing a strong glue bond: the surfaces must be clean and freshly prepared.

Finishing

Although it's the last step in the process, properly preparing your woodworking project and carefully applying a well-chosen finish have a significant payback in the success of the project. Proper preparation includes filling nail holes with wood putty, plugging screw hole counterbores (See above) and thorough finish sanding.

On the following pages you'll find a wealth of woodworking information, along with complete plans for building seven useful, attractive projects. We chose to feature these projects for two reasons: first and foremost, they're creative, well-designed projects that just about anyone would love to own. Second, they represent a wide range of woodworking skills and information. No two projects use the same woods or the exact same joinery, and each one presents a unique challenge. Even if you don't actually build any of these projects (and we think that would be a shame), by reading through the seven chapters, you'll receive a thorough overview of the most important skills a woodworker needs.

Because we know there are many skill levels represented, we arranged this book a little differently than any other woodworking book you may have seen before. The seven chapters each revolve around creating a single woodworking project. If you're a beginning woodworker, we recommend that you read the entire chapter before attempting any of the projects shown. But if you're a little more experienced, we've arranged things so you don't have to waste your time wading through information you may already know. That's why many of the skills we show are presented after the technical illustration and assembly instructions. This way, you can refer back to the information on an as-needed basis.

Whether your interest is in project design, skill-building, or simply using your existing skills to follow a good woodworking plan, you'll find what you're looking for in the following pages.

Pine Bookcase

This simple, elegant bookcase is ideal for beginners and advanced woodworkers alike. It can be built using only standard dimension pine and portable power tools.

- Bookcase design

- Assembling and squaring a carcase

- Making butt joints

- Building a face frame

- Making and installing adjustable shelves

- Painting wood furniture

- Making dowel joints with a doweling jig

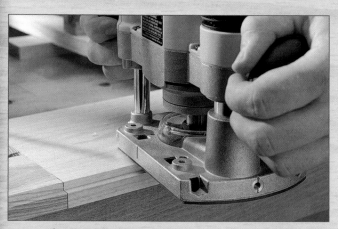

- Cutting rabbets and dadoes with a router

- Making rabbet-and-dado joints

- Making and using a template to cut decorative shapes

Design Features

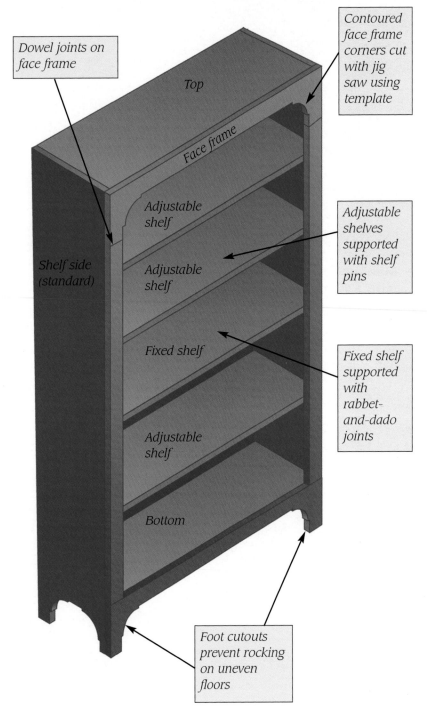

Dowel joints on face frame

Top

Face frame

Contoured face frame corners cut with jig saw using template

Adjustable shelf

Adjustable shelf

Adjustable shelves supported with shelf pins

Shelf side (standard)

Adjustable shelf

Fixed shelf

Fixed shelf supported with rabbet-and-dado joints

Adjustable shelf

Bottom

Foot cutouts prevent rocking on uneven floors

**OVERALL SIZE: 30 IN. WIDE BY
54 IN. TALL BY 10 IN. DEEP**

PROJECT NO. 1:

Pine Bookcase

A bookcase is a great beginning project because it's relatively uncomplicated—it's a box with two sides, a top and a bottom. Shelves are added to hold and display books neatly, and the back strengthens the box and keeps it square. We've added a face frame with decorative cutouts to this bookcase so it looks more like furniture than what it really is—a box.

To make the bookcase even easier to build, it's designed without any moving parts, like doors or drawers. Finally, the bookcase can be built with hand-held power tools—a jig saw and circular saw, a drill and a router.

General planning

Like any other project, building a bookcase involves asking questions about the size, style, materials, design, joinery and general construction and finish before you begin. The considerations are not exclusive of one another—if you want a painted bookcase, for example, you narrow your choices of materials to woods with a straight, tight grain that accepts a painted finish well.

Parts of a bookcase. Any bookcase, regardless of style, will have *shelves* and *sides* (sometimes called *standards*). Shelves may be *fixed,* which are permanently attached to the sides, or *adjustable,* which are generally supported by a system of pins or clips mounted to the shelf sides. The carcase of a small bookcase is generally so sturdy that all the shelves do not have to be integral to the structure—you can simply rest the shelves on clips or dowels inserted into the sides.

Some bookcases, like the one featured in this chapter, include a *back panel* to protect against dust and help keep the bookcase square, and a *face frame* attached to the front of the bookcase to create a more substantive and finished appearance. A bookcase can also include cabinet-style doors. In most cases, bookcase doors feature glass light panels. Many bookcases also have decorative crown-molding style trim surrounding the top and/or the bottom, as well as other decorative embellishments.

Dimensions. When designing a bookcase, start by evaluating the size and number of objects (books or otherwise) that you plan to store in the bookcase. We did some measuring: a standard paperback novel is just over 4 in. wide by about 7 in. tall, so if all we intended to store in our bookcase was paperbacks, we could have built it as shallow as 4 or 5 in. from front to back. But we also wanted to store a set of encyclopedias (each volume is about 8 in. wide and 9½ in. tall) and eventually some 8½- × 11-in. reference books. And on top of that, we hoped to be able to display some picture frames and other *objets d'art* in our bookcase.

From these dimensions we determined that we should build a bookcase at least 9 in. deep and with one or two shelves able to give us clearance of 12 in. or more. The wide variety of our storables suggested that we include at least one or two adjustable shelves in the design.

We decided that a height of about 54 in. would provide room enough for five shelves, and the case would still be short enough to use the top as a display shelf that can be reached easily for dusting.

We hoped to maintain fairly clean lines, so we chose not to add any center shelf supports or shelf stiffeners. That meant that we were limited to a width of about 30 in. (See *Design specs*, right). With our ideal size in mind, we were ready to move on to some more specific considerations, like the type of wood to use.

Material. There are dozens of suitable materials from which you can build a nice bookcase, including such common lumber as pine and oak, as well as veneered plywood. We chose pine because it's easy to work with, relatively inexpensive, and because we planned to paint our bookcase. Pine has a straight grain pattern, which makes it easier for you to obtain a smooth painted finish.

Pine generally is sold with smooth faces and square edges, unlike hardwoods that are usually sold with rough surfaces and edges that require extensive home-shop machining. Pine is sold

About pine

Pine is a *conifer* (it keeps its needle-like vegetation year-round). The species you'll find at most lumber yards grow in various regions of the United States and Canada. In general, the variety of pines that are available to you—*White Pine, Southern Yellow Pine* or *Ponderosa Pine*—share the following characteristics:

Grain: Pine has a straight grain. The grain in Ponderosa and Southern Pine is wider than White Pine, which has the tightest grain of most pine species sold today. Southern Pine can have a coarse texture.

Color: Colors range from light yellow to reddish-brown, depending on the species.

Workability: Pine can blunt cutter edges over time, but otherwise the wood is soft enough that your fingernail can make an impression in the surface, indicating how easy it is to cut and plane. Pine does not bend easily.

Finishing: White Pine and Ponderosa Pine stain more evenly than Southern Pine, but all pine varieties require a wash coat of thinned shellac to help obtain an even stain coat. White Pine and Ponderosa Pine are also excellent for painting. (Birch and poplar, with their tight, straight grain, also are excellent painting woods.)

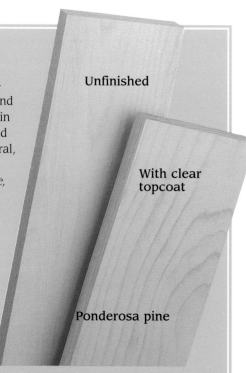

Unfinished

With clear topcoat

Ponderosa pine

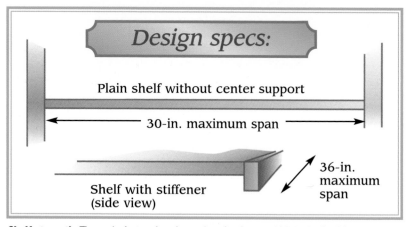

Design specs:

Plain shelf without center support

30-in. maximum span

Shelf with stiffener (side view)

36-in. maximum span

Shelf strength. The main factor that determines bookcase width is the load-bearing capacity of the shelves. A ¾-in.-thick board with no center support or stiffeners can span about 30 in. before it begins to sag under the weight of its load. This limits the width of the bookcase to about 30 in. You can make a bookcase wider than 30 in. if you add vertical partitions to provide center support for the shelves, or if you reinforce the shelf fronts with stiffeners. Doubling-up the shelf material and adding cleats beneath the joints between the shelves and the sides are two more ways to increase shelf strength. Just be sure your sides are strong enough to support the extra weight, as well.

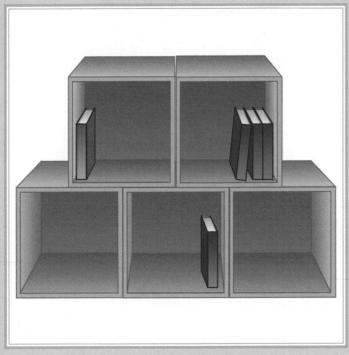

Modular bookcases consist of several components, usually box-shaped, that can be stacked and restacked to meet your storage needs. Although they consist of several separate units, the better-designed versions give the appearance of a solid piece of furniture when stacked together.

Accent bookcases can be custom-built to fit small spaces. The small Arts-and-Crafts bookcase shown here would be an effective addition to a room already containing other furnishings with a similar style.

Nominal vs. actual wood dimensions:	
Nom. size (in.)	Actual size (in.)
1 × 2	¾ × 1½
1 × 3	¾ × 2½
1 × 4	¾ × 3½
1 × 6	¾ × 5¼
1 × 8	¾ × 7¼
1 × 10	¾ × 9¼
1 × 12	¾ × 11¼
1 × 14	¾ × 13¼

dimensionally—a 1 × 10 board is actually ¾ × 9¼ in. (See *chart,* left). We decided to use 1×10 (actually 9¼ in. wide) to give us a bookcase that had just about the depth we were looking for. Because our bookcase would be painted, we weren't concerned about the appearance of the wood in the back panel. So we chose lauan plywood—an inexpensive Philippine mahogany.

Aesthetics. Once the factors of engineering, efficiency and practicality are dealt with, you can begin to consider aesthetics. Evaluating proportion and decoration does not come easily to everyone. If you have no formal design training (as is the case with many successful woodworkers), simply look at other bookcases, refer to furniture catalogs or bring a tape measure to a local furniture store.

Incorporate the dimensions and other ideas that you like into your own design.

The scrolled pattern in our bookcase sides and face frame is borrowed from a bookcase designed by George Hepplewhite, the 18th-century designer who, along with Chippendale and Sheraton, influenced generations of furniture makers. The simple scroll cuts refine an otherwise ordinary box.

Construction details

Because a bookcase is so simple structurally, you have quite a few options when it comes to issues like joinery techniques and adding decorative embellishments.

Joinery. The appropriate types of wood joinery to use for your project depends on how strong the bookcase needs to be and

A bookcase with drawers increases your storage options. Positioned in the cavity normally used as the bottom shelf, the drawers do not cause the bookcase to take on the look of a cupboard. The design above also includes a draw-curtain to keep dust out of the bookcase.

Cabinet-style bookcases include doors, usually with glass panels. They offer good protection for rare books or collectibles and make a great addition to any study or den.

how formal or finished you want it to look. Since most of the load is carried by the joints between the fixed shelves and the sides, these are the most important joints. For a light-duty bookcase that will be used in a utility area, you can probably get by with something as simple as butt joints reinforced with glue and screws, although you may want to add shelf cleats beneath the joints. But for greater strength, many bookcases are built using dado joints cut into the sides to hold the shelves.

A third and much less common option is the dado-rabbet joint (See *Dado-rabbet joints,* page 28). This joint is made by cutting narrow dadoes into the sides to accept rabbeted shelf ends. It is an especially good joint for the top and bottom of the bookcase because it interlocks these parts with the sides, unlike the straight rabbet joint where the joint is unsupported on the top or bottom.

The other primary stress points on a bookcase are the face frame corners (if your design includes a face

frame). We chose to use dowel joints at these points (See *Dowel joints,* page 30). Biscuit joints are another good option for constructing face frames.

Finally, we recessed the ¼-in.-thick back panel into a ¼-in.-deep rabbet cut on the inside edges of the back of the bookcase.

Decorative elements. Adding the right decorative touches can transform an ordinary project into an interesting showpiece. And sometimes the decorative features can have a practical application as well. The contoured cutouts at the bottoms of the face frame and sides, for example, create "feet" that make the bookcase more stable on an uneven surface. Like the cutouts on the top of the face frame, they were made by first creating a pattern template (See FIGURE E, page 24), then following the template with a jig saw.

The face frame itself is assembled as a separate unit, then attached to the bookcase with finish nails and wood glue.

PINE BOOKCASE

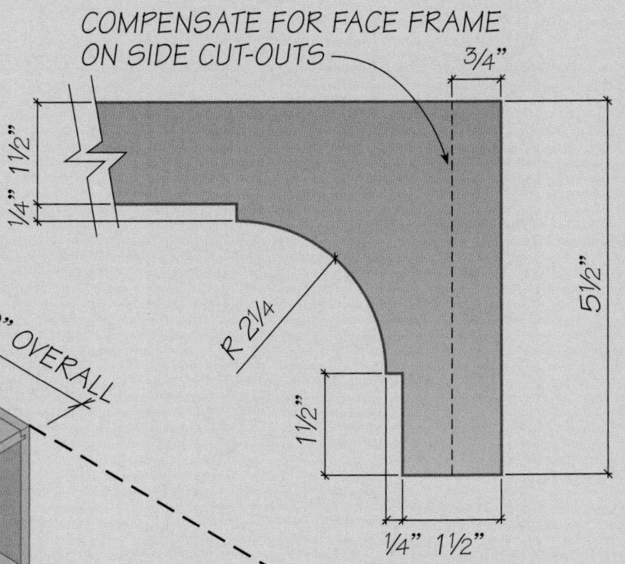
FACE FRAME RAIL/SIDE BASE PATTERN
COMPENSATE FOR FACE FRAME ON SIDE CUT-OUTS
3/4"
1 1/2"
1/4"
R 2 1/4
5 1/2"
1 1/2"
1/4" 1 1/2"

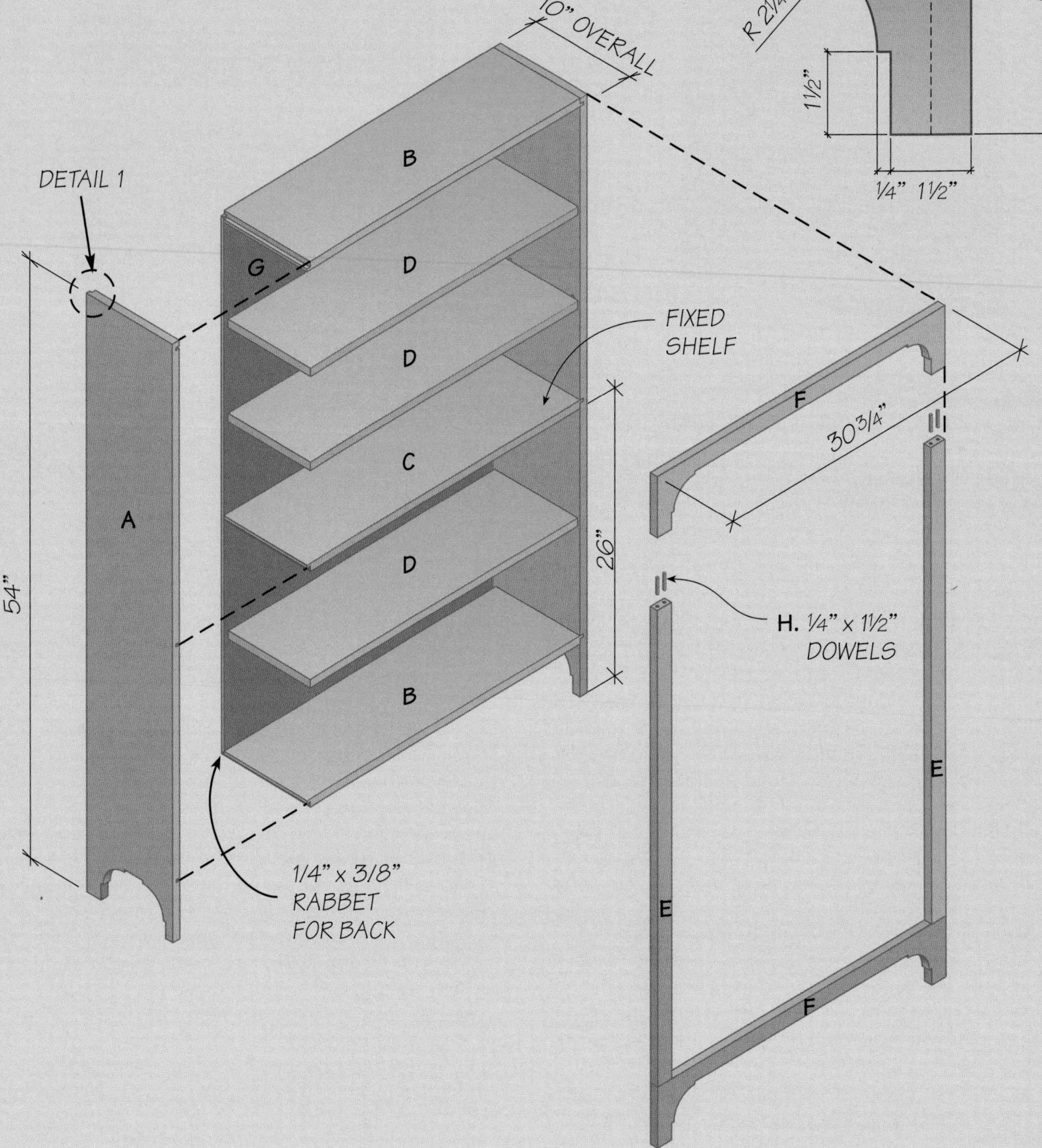
10" OVERALL
DETAIL 1
B
G
D
D
FIXED SHELF
C
A
D
26"
54"
B
1/4" x 3/8" RABBET FOR BACK
F
30 3/4"
H. 1/4" x 1 1/2" DOWELS
E
E
F

Pine Bookcase Cutting List

Part		No.	Size	Material
A.	Sides	2	¾ × 9¼ × 54"	Pine
B.	Top, Bottom	2	¾ × 9¼ × 30"	"
C.	Fixed Shelf	1	¾ × 9 × 30"	"
D.	Adjustable Shelves	3	¾ × 9 × 29⅛"	"
E.	Face Frame Stiles	2	¾ × 1½ × 43"	"
F.	Face Frame Rails	2	¾ × 5½ × 30¾"	"
G.	Back	1	¼ × 30 × 48½"	Lauan Plywood
H.	Face Frame Fasteners	8	¼ dia. × 1½" long	Spiral-grooved Dowel

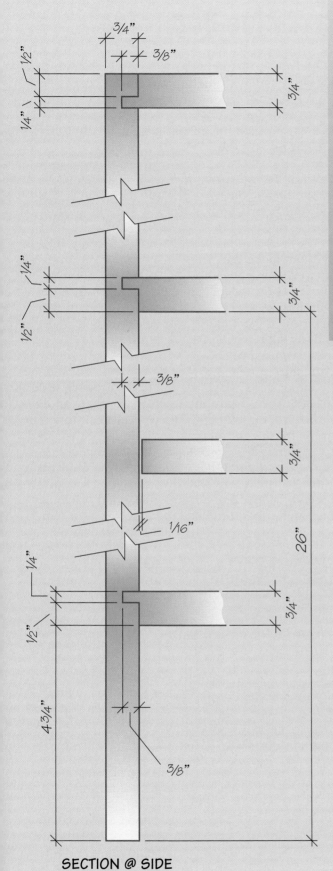

SECTION @ SIDE

DETAIL I:
RABBETS ON
SIDES, TOP
AND BOTTOM
FOR BACK

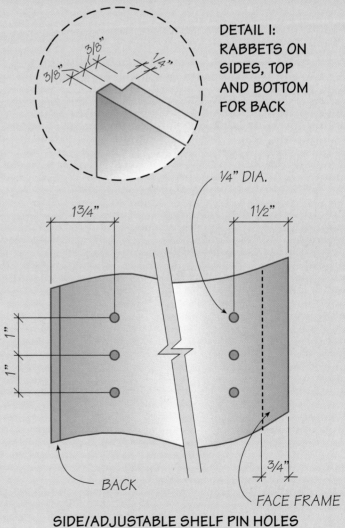

SIDE/ADJUSTABLE SHELF PIN HOLES

Project Assembly Steps: Pine Bookcase

Build the sides

1 Begin by selecting the 1×10 boards you'll use for each of the carcase parts—sides, top, bottom, and so forth—and label the parts.

2 Cross-cut the sides to length.

3 Cut three dadoes on each side—one for the top, one for the bottom, and one for the fixed shelf. We used a router (See *Dadoes & rabbets*, page 26), but you can use your table saw, if you prefer, by installing a dado-blade set or simply making multiple passes with a rip-cutting blade. The tricky part of this operation is making sure the dadoes in each side are aligned. To ensure proper alignment when using a router, clamp the sides together, edge-to-edge, with the top and bottom edges flush. Clamp a straightedge cutting guide to the workpieces as a guide for your router. To make the dadoes specified for this project, chuck a ¼-in. straight bit into the router and set the depth of the cut to ⅜ in. Then make each dado cut across both sides in one pass.

FIGURE A: The cutout contour for the bottoms of the sides can be drawn using a template made from the dimensions shown above and the drawing, p. 20.

10-in. wide
2-in. radius
1½-in. wide

4 Next, make the scroll-sawn foot cutouts in the sides. There are several methods you can use to draw your cutting lines. We used a template pattern (See *Templates*, page 29). You can use the dimensions shown on the detail drawing **(See FIGURE A)** to create the template, or you can draw the pattern directly onto the workpieces. NOTE: The profile for the cutouts on the bottoms of the sides is the same as the profile for the *face frame rail/base pattern* on page 20, except the radius is 2 in. for the sides, not 2¼. If you use this second method, lay out and cut one side, sand or file out the rough spots, then use the first side as a template for tracing the cutout onto the other side. Make the cutouts with a scroll saw or jig saw.

5 Bore the adjustable shelf pin holes in each side. We used a piece of perforated hardboard as a guide to drill pin holes that are 1 in. apart on-center (See *TIP*, left). If you prefer, you can carefully plot out the centerpoint for each hole using a straightedge, or make a plywood drilling guide on your drill press. We also attached a right angle drilling guide to our drill to ensure that

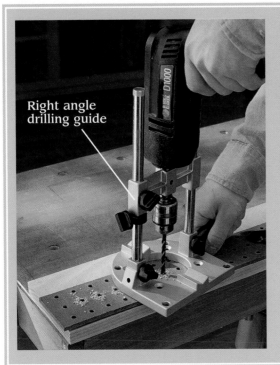

Right angle drilling guide

TIP: Make a drilling guide from perforated hardboard

A narrow piece of perforated hardboard (pegboard) makes drilling evenly spaced holes quick and easy. Simply mark a centerpoint for your top or bottom hole, according to your construction plans, then clamp the perfboard to your workpiece, making sure one of the holes in the perfboard falls over the centerpoint. Be sure the edge of the perfboard is parallel to the line you want the holes to follow, then start drilling. Use a depth stop on your drill—in the photo to the left, we're using a right angle drill guide to ensure that the holes are perpendicular. *NOTE: Use tempered perfboard for an accurate and durable guide.*

the dowel pin holes are perpendicular. Make sure to clamp the drilling guide to the workpieces with the same orientation and starting point for each side so that the holes will match.

Cut the shelves, top and bottom

1 Lay out and cross-cut the fixed shelf, top and bottom to length. Reset and cut the adjustable shelves to length. (They're ¾ in. shorter than the other cross members because they won't have the ⅜ in. rabbet ledge on each end.)

2 Rip-cut the fixed shelf and the adjustable shelves to a width of 9 in. (The shelves are ¼ in. narrower than the sides, top and bottom to allow for the thickness of the back panel.)

3 Double-check the width and depth of the dadoes in the sides (for the project as shown, ¼ in. wide × ⅜ in. deep), and lay out matching rabbets on the ends of the top, bottom and fixed shelf using a try square. Cut the rabbets with a router and a ¼-in. straight bit (See *Dado-rabbet joints*, page 28), or use your table saw.

4 Using a router or a table saw, cut a ⅜-in.-wide × ¼-in.-deep rabbet groove in one long edge of each of the sides, as well as the top and bottom. These will create a recess for the back panel when the carcase is assembled. *NOTE: You can also make the recess cuts by routing the inside of the opening after the carcase is assembled, then squaring the corners of the cut with a chisel.*

Assemble the carcase

1 Dry-assemble the sides, fixed shelf, top and bottom to make sure the parts fit together correctly. Make adjustments, if needed.

2 Lay the sides edge-to-edge on a flat worksurface, with the dadoes facing up, and align the dadoes. Squeeze a bead of glue across both sides into the dadoes at the top and bottom of

FIGURE B: Use a pair of pipe clamps or bar clamps at the top and another pair at the bottom. Wood cauls at the outsides of the joint distribute the clamping pressure more evenly while protecting the surfaces of the wood from the clamp heads.

each side. Spread the glue evenly with a brush or glue stick. Apply glue to the rabbet ledges on the top and bottom.

3 Fit the top and bottom into the dadoes in the side to form the carcase assembly. Apply a pair of pipe clamps or bar clamps to the joint at the top and the bottom. We used 9-in.-long wood *cauls* at each joint to protect the bookcase sides and distribute the clamp force more evenly **(See FIGURE B)**. Tighten the clamps until the joints are flush—be careful not to apply too much clamping pressure.

FIGURE C: Measure the diagonals of the bookcase carcase to see if it's square. Adjust the carcase by shifting the clamps until the diagonal measurements are the same. Be careful not to disturb the carcase while the glue sets up.

FIGURE D: After the carcase is assembled and the glue has dried, glue and clamp the fixed shelf into the dadoes in the sides. Wax paper placed beneath the joints keeps the project from bonding to your worksurface.

4 Check the cabinet for square by measuring the diagonals **(See FIGURE C)**. If the measurements are not equal, shift the top or bottom until the diagonals are the same. This can take a few tries—just try to get the carcase squared up before the glue begins to set (about 10 minutes or so with most yellow wood glue). Let the glue dry for at least one hour before proceeding with the carcase assembly. *TIP: Wipe up any glue squeeze-out on the carcase members with a damp sponge.*

5 Test-fit the fixed shelf in the dadoes in the centers of the sides. If you need to use force to get the shelf to fit, lightly sand the ends of the rabbet ledges—a fixed shelf that's even slightly too long can create undue tension in the carcase and could also cause bowing in the sides (this is why we waited until after the top and bottom had been squared and attached to the sides to install the fixed shelf).

6 Glue and clamp the fixed shelf in place **(See FIGURE D)**. Make sure the front of the shelf is flush with the front of the carcase, and the back is flush with the shoulder of the recess at the back of the carcase (you may want to insert ¼-in. temporary spacers beneath the shelf if the carcase is lying on its back).

Install the back panel

1 Measure the height and width of the recess opening at the back of the carcase. Be sure to measure from the shoulders of the rabbets.

2 Cut the back panel so it's square and slightly smaller than the recess opening. We used inexpensive ¼-in. lauan plywood for the back, since we planned to paint the bookcase.

3 Apply a thin bead of glue to the rabbeted recess, then place the back panel into the recess. The glue alone should be strong enough to hold the panel in place, but you can reinforce the joints with a few wire nails if it makes you more comfortable.

Build and attach the face frame

1 Although we provide exact dimensions for the face frame members, be sure to take accurate top-to-bottom and left-to-right measurements from the actual bookcase before cutting the face frame parts. This guarantees a flush fit.

2 Measure and cut the face frame rails and stiles to size.

3 Use a template to lay out the corner patterns in the top and bottom rails (See *Transfer patterns,* page 134). The rails are cut from 1×6 pine. Although this creates some waste, it's easier than cutting the corners separately and assembling the parts. **FIGURE E** provides a grid pattern for making

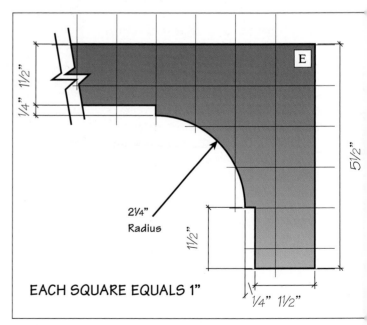

EACH SQUARE EQUALS 1"

FIGURE E: You can use this scale grid drawing to make a template for cutting the face frame contours, or simply use the dimensions from the detail drawing on page 20.

the template, or you can use the dimensions from the detail drawing on page 20 *(face frame rail pattern)*.

4 Make the contour cuts on the face frame rails by using a jig saw or scroll saw to follow the layout lines **(See FIGURE F).**

5 Join the face frame rails and stiles with doweled butt joints and glue (See *Dowel joints,* page 30*)*.

6 Clamp the assembly with two bar or pipe clamps (one parallel to each stile). Use a clamp pad between the wood and each clamp jaw so the jaw doesn't mar the wood.

7 Check the face frame assembly for square by measuring the diagonals, as you did with the carcase.

8 When the face frame glue dries, glue and nail it to the cabinet with 1½-in. finishing nails driven into pilot holes **(See FIGURE G).** Set the nail heads below the surface with a nailset.

9 Sand the joints between the face frame and the carcase if the surfaces are uneven.

Finishing touches

1 Once the carcase is assembled and the glue is dry, fill the nail holes (where the face-frame was installed) and the joint seams with paintable wood filler putty. Putty that resists shrinkage is best. Let the putty set up for as long as the instructions require, then sand the putty smooth with 100-grit sandpaper. If there are still gaps at the joints, repeat the process.

2 Sand all surfaces with 100- or 150-grit, then 180-grit sandpaper.

3 Wipe the surfaces clean, then apply your finish of choice. We used primer and enamel paint (See *Painting furniture,* pages 32 to 33).

4 Paint a length of ¼-in.-dia. hardwood dowel for the adjustable

shelf pins. (A good way to paint dowels is to insert one end into a dowel hole in a piece of scrap wood so the dowel stands upright.) Cut the dowel into 1-in.-long pins after the paint dries, and insert the dowels into the dowel holes in the sides at the appropriate heights. Touch up the cut ends with a little paint, then rest the adjustable shelves on the pins.

FIGURE F: Using a hardboard template (See Templates, page 29) helps ensure that the cutouts are the same in all workpieces. Make the cuts with a jig saw fitted with a scrolling blade. Clamp a straightedge to the workpiece and use it as a cutting guide for making the long, straight portions of the cuts.

FIGURE G: The face frame for the bookcase, as with most other cabinets, is assembled separately, then attached to the front with glue and finish nails. Even with softwoods like pine, be sure to drill pilots holes for the finish nails—it would be a real shame to split any of the parts after putting so much work into them. If you don't have a drill bit small enough to make the pilot holes, cut the head off one of the finish nails, chuck it in the drill, and use the nail as a drill bit.

WOODWORKING SKILLS
Cutting dadoes & rabbets

Dadoes and rabbets are fundamental to wood joinery. Technically, a dado is a square groove cut across the grain of a workpiece. Grooves cut with the grain are often mistakenly called dadoes as well, but in fact they're known as plows. A rabbet is an open groove cut at the end of a workpiece.

There are several ways to go about cutting dadoes and rabbets. Long ago, they were most commonly made with hand planes containing chisels the same thickness as the cut being made. Today, most woodworkers use a router with a straight bit to cut dadoes and plows, and sometimes rabbets. Rabbets can also be cut with a piloted bit that's used without a straightedge. Another option is to use a table saw or radial arm saw equipped with a special dado-cutting blade set. In some cases, it's easier to make the cuts simply by making multiple passes with an ordinary circular saw blade.

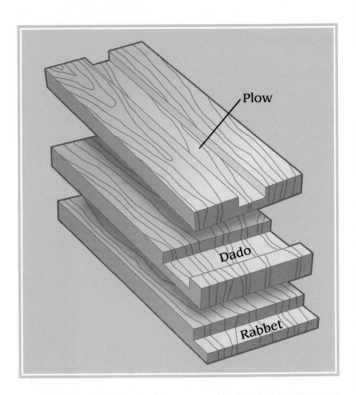

Cutting dadoes with a router & straight bit

A router guide is needed to make a dado or plow with a straight router bit. The simplest guide is a plain, straight board clamped to the workpiece the correct distance from the cutting line, as in the photo above. For rough work, sliding attachments that fit onto the router base may be used as a guide. Select a bit with a diameter equal to the desired width of the dado. Make the cut in multiple passes of increasing depth to avoid bogging down the motor. Move the router from left to right.

Cutting rabbets with a router & straight bit

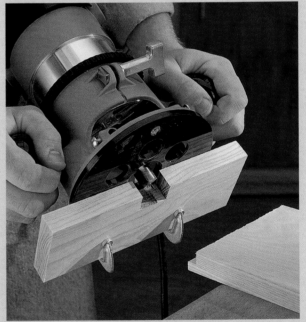

Clamping a wood guide to the router base is a quick and easy way to use a straight bit for making rabbet cuts. Cut a recess in one edge of the board to house the spinning bit, then clamp the board to the base so the cutting edge of the bit extends past the guide an amount equal to the planned width of the rabbet. As with dadoes, avoid cutting too much stock at once by making multiple passes until the desired depth is achieved.

Dadoes & rabbets

Plow

Dado

Rabbet

HOW TO CUT A RABBET GROOVE WITH A PILOTED RABBET BIT

Piloted rabbet bit

1 Install a router bit with a piloted arbor in your router. Pilots with bearings, like the one shown here, cut more cleanly with less burning than fixed pilots.

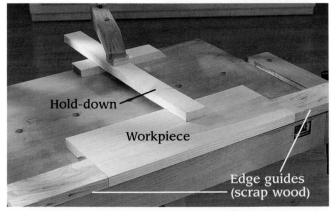
Hold-down
Workpiece
Edge guides
(scrap wood)

2 Set up for the cut by securing your workpiece to the worksurface. A good method is to clamp a hold-down to the opposite edge of the worksurface, as in the photo above. Make sure the edge of the work-piece to be routed extends past the edge of the worksurface slightly. Also clamp a piece of scrap wood the same thickness as the workpiece at each end of the workpiece, flush with the front edge. These scrap pieces prevent the piloted router bit from following the corner of the workpiece.

3 With the bit in place and set to the proper cutting depth, engage the router. After it has built up to full speed, apply it to the wood scrap to start the cut. Draw the router toward yourself at an even pace, making sure the pilot maintains contact with the edge of the workpiece and the router base stays flat on the surface. Cut well past the end of the workpiece and into the scrap before withdrawing the bit. Allow the bit to wind down completely before setting down the router or adjusting the cutting depth.

OPTION: Dado-blade sets

Chippers

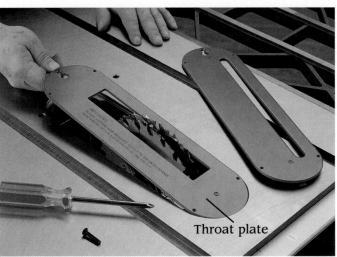
Throat plate

A dado-blade set is a popular saw accessory used to cut dadoes, rabbets and plows. The dado set can be used with a table saw or a radial arm saw. It consists of a pair of ordinary circular blades that sandwich sets of chippers—you adjust the width of the cut by adding or removing chippers. When mounted in a table saw, dado-blade sets require a saw throat plate with an extra-wide opening.

WOODWORKING SKILLS
Making a dado-rabbet joint

Dadoes and rabbets can be used individually to create highly useful wood joints. Or, you can combine the two to make a dado-rabbet joint that exploits the best qualities of each joint type.

A dado-rabbet joint is formed when the rabbeted end or edge of a workpiece is fitted into a dado groove in the mating workpiece. In combining the two joint types, the result is a joint that is interlocking to a greater degree than either joint alone. And you increase the surface area covered by glue, which strengthens the glue bond of the joint.

Dado-rabbet joints are especially useful in carcase construction. When used to join the top and bottom to the sides of a carcase, dado-rabbet joints hide more end grain and allow the carcase to be dry-assembled more easily and accurately.

Cut the dadoes first, then use the actual thickness of each dado joint as a guide for cutting the rabbets.

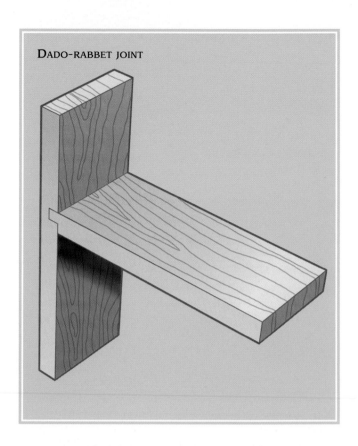

DADO-RABBET JOINT

HOW TO MAKE A DADO-RABBET JOINT

1 Cut the dadoes at the joint locations using a straight router bit or a table saw and dado-blade set (See OPTION, page 27). Measure the thickness of the dadoes and use the measurement as a guide for cutting rabbets with lips that fit exactly into the dadoes. Make sure the rabbeted ends will not extend more than halfway into the dadoed board. We used a straight router bit with a straightedge guide attached to the router base to cut the rabbets.

2 Test-fit the joints and adjust the thickness of the rabbet ledge by trimming, if needed. Apply glue to both surfaces and assemble and clamp the joint.

HOW TO MAKE PARTS WITH A TEMPLATE

1 Work out a full-scale version of the desired pattern on graph paper. If your plan includes a grid drawing, use it as a basis for enlarging the pattern to scale. Once the drawing is complete to your satisfaction, cut it out with a utility knife or scissors. Next, tape the pattern to a piece of hardboard and trace the pattern with a felt-tipped pen.

2 Cut out the template shape on the hardboard, using a jig saw or scroll saw. Smooth the edges with a rasp and sandpaper. Lay the template in position on the workpiece and trace it with a pencil.

3 With a jig saw or scroll saw, cut slightly on the waste side of the line. For corners or small-radius curves, it may not be possible to make the cut in one continuous pass. You'll need to make several access cuts through the waste area and up to the cutting line.

WOODWORKING SKILLS
Making & using a template

Templates are layout guides used to ensure uniform cuts when making multiple workpieces. While most woodworking stores and catalogs sell numerous templates used to trace common woodworking shapes and contours, learning to make your own will greatly expand the range of cuts you can make.

If you're working from a plan drawing, more complex projects likely will include detailed information about their dimensions and profiles. This may be in the form of a scaled drawing with spacing and curve radii called out, or it could be a drawing of the shape overlaid on a scaled grid. Or, you can invent shapes and contours of your own and create templates for them. Whatever the source, the only materials you need to make templates are graph paper, some scrap hardboard or acrylic, and a few simple hand tools.

4 Once the pattern is cut, use a smoothing rasp to remove excess wood up to the cutting line. Sand the contours smooth.
NOTE: Although you can use the contoured workpiece itself as a template, stick to using the hardboard template for consistent results.

WOODWORKING SKILLS
Making dowel joints with a doweling jig

Dowel joints are reinforced butt joints that are used frequently for edge gluing and frame building—especially face frames used in cabinet construction. They increase the strength of a joint and, when used carefully, assist in the alignment of the mating workpieces. Today, they're not used as commonly as in years past due to the advent of the biscuit joiner. But for those who don't own a biscuit joiner, they're still essential to wood joinery. And unlike biscuits, dowels can be added after the joint is assembled.

There are three basic types of dowel joint: the *hidden dowel joint,* the *through dowel joint,* and the *stopped dowel joint.* The best method for making a dowel joint depends on the type of joint you're making and on the equipment you've got on hand. Commercially produced doweling jigs, like the one shown here, are designed for making highly accurate hidden dowel joints for reinforcing butt joints or edge gluing. Dowel points (round metal spurs that fit into a dowel hole) can be used instead to transfer the exact location of the dowel hole centerpoint to the mating workpiece.

Because alignment is so important, use a drill press whenever possible. If using a portable drill, it's a good idea to attach a right angle drill guide to ensure straight, perpendicular dowel holes.

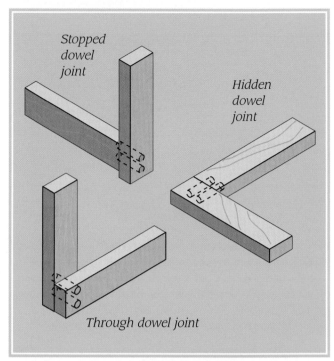

The three most common dowel joints are the hidden dowel joint, the through dowel joint, and the stopped dowel joint. Hidden dowel joints are used purely for reinforcement and alignment, and are the trickiest of the three types to make. Through dowel joints are formed by driving a dowel into a hole drilled all the way through two mating parts. Stopped dowel joints are made by drilling through one joint member and partway into the other, then driving a dowel into the hole and trimming the end flush with the exposed surface. Through dowel joints and stopped dowel joints often are used to add a decorative element to a design.

HOW TO MAKE A DOWEL JOINT WITH A DOWELING JIG

1 To lay out the dowel joints, butt the two mating parts together, making sure the mating surfaces are flush. Mark the dowel hole locations by drawing a single line across the joint for each dowel. For best results, use at least two evenly spaced dowels at each joint.

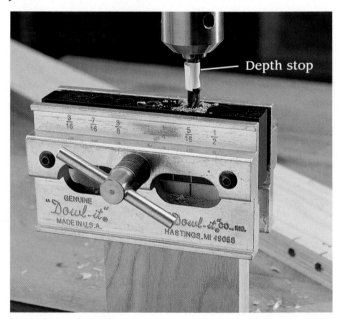

2 Slip the doweling jig over each mating edge. Align the mark on the jig corresponding to the diameter of the dowel hole with each location line you drew on the workpiece. Drill a dowel hole the same diameter as the dowel at each mark—use a depth stop to keep holes uniform.

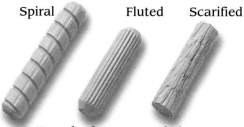

Spiral   Fluted   Scarified

Dowels shown actual size

Dowels for making dowel joints include pre-fabricated dowel pins, like the *spiral dowel* and the *fluted dowel* above, or simply pieces of hardwood doweling. The grooves in the fluted and spiral dowels provide space for the glue to lodge during assembly, increasing the durability of the joint. By scarifying a plain hardwood dowel with the jaws of a pliers, as in the dowel on the right above, you can approximate the same effect.

Hardwood doweling

½ in. ⅜ in. ¼ in.

Hardwood doweling has one main advantage: it's available in a wider range of diameters. Choose dowels with a diameter one-half the thickness of the workpieces.

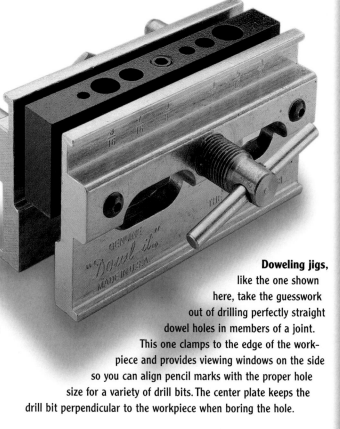

Doweling jigs, like the one shown here, take the guesswork out of drilling perfectly straight dowel holes in members of a joint. This one clamps to the edge of the workpiece and provides viewing windows on the side so you can align pencil marks with the proper hole size for a variety of drill bits. The center plate keeps the drill bit perpendicular to the workpiece when boring the hole.

3 After drilling all the holes, apply a dab of glue into each hole. Also apply glue to the mating wood surfaces. Slide the dowels into the holes to make the joint.

4 Create all the joints, then clamp the assembly together with pipe clamps or bar clamps. Be sure to use a clamp pad between the wood and the clamp jaws so the jaws don't mar the wood. Do not overtighten the clamps.

Painting furniture

Painted furniture is often underrated, with current preferences running toward retaining natural wood tones. But the fact is, there are some types of furniture, and some types of wood, that actually look better painted. The key, as with any finish, is to choose good finishing products and apply them carefully and correctly.

While latex-based paints are less toxic and easier to clean up than their oil-based counterparts, most furnituremakers still prefer oil-based products. Enamel oil-based paint dries to create a very hard protective surface. It's also easier to create a smooth finish with oil-based paints. Still, if you prefer working with latex paints, you can get reasonably good results as long as you use an enamel primer.

Woods with narrow, tight grain, such as birch and poplar, work best for painting. Pine is also a frequent choice for painted furniture: it takes the paint well, and you're not paying for wood with good figure just to cover it up with paint.

Supplies for painting furniture include: sandpaper; wood putty for filling voids, nail and screw holes, and wood defects; oil-based enamel paint; primer/sealer; a paint roller for broad surfaces; and sponge brushes for smooth paint application.

HOW TO PAINT FURNITURE

1 Fill nail holes or screw holes, knots and other surface defects with paintable wood filler putty. Apply the putty so its surface is slightly higher than the surrounding wood surface when dry.

2 Sand the filled areas so they're smooth and level with the surrounding wood. For most projects, use 100- or 150-grit sandpaper to remove the excess material, then sand with 180-grit sandpaper to remove rough spots and sanding marks. Wipe the surface thoroughly with a damp rag or a tack cloth.

Painting furniture

3 Apply a thin coat of primer/sealer. Primer/sealer helps the paint bond more evenly, and forms a protective layer to prevent agents within the wood from seeping out and causing stains in the painted surface. It's not critical, but generally you should use oil-based primer with oil-based paint. NOTE: Instead of commercial primer/sealer, some woodworkers prefer to use a mixture of thinned orange shellac and boiled linseed oil for the primer coat.

4 Scuff the primed surface lightly with 180- or 220-grit sandpaper after the primer dries. This creates "tooth" on the surface so the paint will bond better. Be sure to wipe the primed surface with a tack cloth or damp rag before applying the first coat of paint.

5 Apply a thin, even coat of enamel oil-based paint to all surfaces. The most common mistake made when painting is to apply layers that are too thick. An overly heavy coat of paint can sag and dry unevenly. If you can't see the primer coat at all through the first coat of paint, you've probably applied too much paint.

6 Apply the next coat. As a rule, let the first coat dry overnight no matter what the paint can tells you: a chief cause of paint failure is moisture trapped between coats. Apply additional coats, scuff sanding lightly between coats. Three to four thin coats should yield a fine painted finish.

Shaker-style Valet Table

This compact table fits neatly into a foyer or hallway, where it provides a warm welcome to all. It features a generous surface area for keys, mail or a favorite photo, and a handy drawer for gloves, scarves and other small items. The pleasing design is based on the popular Shaker style with its trim, no-nonsense lines and sturdy maple construction. Because this timeless valet table is so simple in design, it can fit into just about any decor—and it doesn't take ages to build.

Woodworking Skills You'll Learn:

- Edge-gluing wood panels
- Cutting tenons
- Cutting a stopped mortise
- Attaching a tabletop
- Building a five-board interlocking drawer
- Hanging a flush drawer on wooden drawer slides

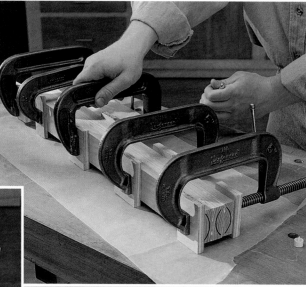

• Laminating wood stock

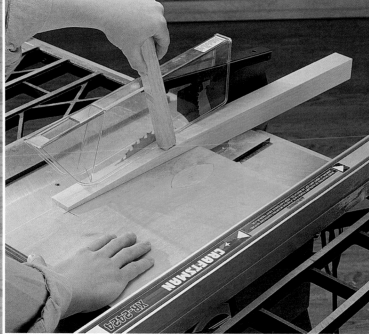

• Cutting tapers with a tapering jig

• Applying a natural wood finish

• Making pinned mortise-and-tenon joints

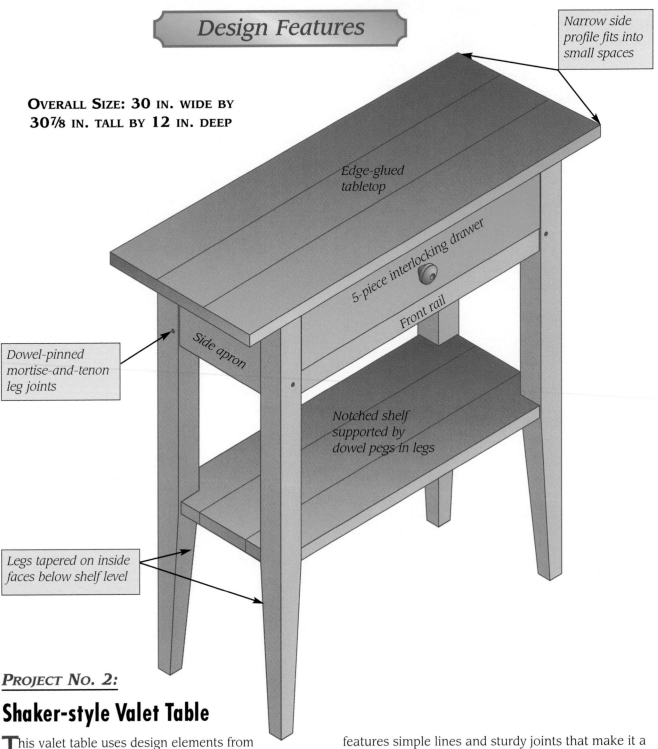

Design Features

OVERALL SIZE: 30 IN. WIDE BY 30⅞ IN. TALL BY 12 IN. DEEP

Narrow side profile fits into small spaces

Edge-glued tabletop

5-piece interlocking drawer

Front rail

Side apron

Dowel-pinned mortise-and-tenon leg joints

Notched shelf supported by dowel pegs in legs

Legs tapered on inside faces below shelf level

PROJECT NO. 2:

Shaker-style Valet Table

This valet table uses design elements from the classic Shaker furniture style to create a trim, attractive project for your foyer or hallway. Because it's a mere 12 in. deep from front to back, the valet table can be nestled snugly against a wall in areas where floor space is at a premium. The broad drawer creates a convenient storage spot for gloves or other items you normally grab as you leave the house. And the tabletop makes a great resting spot for keys, mail and other items you bring into the house.

Made of hard maple, the Shaker-style valet table

features simple lines and sturdy joints that make it a highly durable home furnishing. The distinctly Shaker characteristics include legs that are square on top and tapered on the inside faces, mortise-and-tenon joinery, a center-hung drawer and an overhanging tabletop.

Building this valet table will help you improve several important woodworking skills, including gluing-up hardwood stock, cutting tapers, making mortise-and-tenon joints and building drawers. If the table shown here is not the right size for your space, the small number of parts used makes the plan easy to modify.

General planning

When you're building furniture for tight areas, it's best to start the planning process by measuring the space where the project will be installed. If you plan to use the valet table in a hallway or foyer, measure the area and make sure that any design will leave at least 32 in. of clear walking space. If the valet table won't fit into either of these spaces, you can put it just about anywhere: in the kitchen near the door; in the bedroom as a nightstand; in a dining room as a stand for your silverware cask. It's a versatile design with many options.

Parts of a valet table. The business end of this table is the overhanging *tabletop*, which in this case is made of edge-glued boards. Three *aprons* support the sides and back of the tabletop from below. Tapered *legs* provide support and decorative lines. The *drawer* is made using interlocking joints. It's supported by two wooden *drawer guide assemblies* that attach to the inside faces of the side aprons and serve as drawer runners. A *front rail* directly below the drawer front provides lateral strength and the appearance of a face frame for the drawer. A removable *shelf* rests between the legs on dowel pins above each leg taper.

Dimensions. This valet table is 30⅞ in. tall, 30 in. wide and a 12 in. deep to fit unobtrusively in an entry hall. The tabletop extends only ½ in. beyond the front to provide full access to the drawer. The 1-in. overhang at the back accommodates baseboard molding, allowing the tabletop to fit flush to the wall.

Material. We used hard maple to build most of the valet table—one of the three most common woods used in Shaker-style furniture (the others are cherry and birch). The only non-maple parts are the drawer glide system, the tabletop cleats and the sides, back and bottom of the drawer. These are made of ¾-in. pine, except the lauan plywood drawer bottom.

Aesthetics. Shaker-style furniture is admired for the lack of adornment that separates it from most other furniture styles. Even the decorative elements the Shakers incorporated into their furniture, such as tapered legs, are simple and have a functional component. The tapers visually lighten the proportions of the furniture legs, but they also create more leg

About maple

Along with red oak, maple is the most common woodworking wood today, due to its desirability and its availability. Most home building centers stock hard maple in premilled dimensional sizes, and lumberyards sell maple either rough or planed on one or more surfaces.

Grain: Maple has a straight, tight grain, although it's not uncommon to find wavy patterns even in a relatively straight-grained piece. You'll also find curly or bird's eye patterns caused by irregular growths. These (bird's eye and curly or fiddleback) are considered the most desirable maple varieties, and are relatively rare and costly—although it's becoming easier to find them in more affordable veneer form.

Color: Colors range from white at the outer growth, or sapwood, to reddish brown heartwood. When finished, maple usually acquires a slight yellow or orange cast (think of gym floors or bowling alleys).

Workability: Even where the grain is straight, maple can be difficult to cut and plane. It's not uncommon for power tool cutters to leave burn marks on hard maple. The unpredictable wavy or figured grain in a board with mostly straight grain can cause a planer blade to tear out the wood.

Unfinished

With clear topcoat

Hard maple

Design specs

HALLWAY

Minimum 32-in. clear walkway

Whether you may safely position furnishings in a hallway depends upon the width of the hallway. As a rule, leave at least 32 in. of clear walking space between the opposite wall and the furniture you add. Base your design on the available space in excess of 32 in.

A bistro table with a marble top and carved, tapered legs can convert a plain entry into a formal reception area.

This upright Arts-and-Crafts-style server is designed as dining room furniture, but in the right entry or hallway it makes a dramatic valet table.

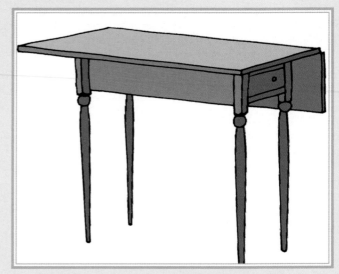

A drop-leaf table with a narrow centerboard fits neatly against the wall for everyday use. On special occasions, it can be set up elsewhere in the home for serving refreshments.

Adding a back with mirrored glass and coat hooks converts an ordinary valet table into a multi-use piece of furniture that visitors are sure to appreciate.

A library-style table can be adapted to fit into a narrow space, without loss of style and function, by shrinking the front-to-back dimension.

room and access, particularly on larger pieces of furniture like dining tables. Shaker table legs typically are square at the top, then taper below the aprons and front rail. Unlike the four-sided leg tapers of their day, however, Shakers tapered only the two inside faces, leaving the outside faces square (after all, there's no practical reason to taper the outside faces). Because our valet table has a lower shelf, we started the leg tapers below the shelf height to avoid attaching the legs at an angle.

The drawer face and the rail below it are cut from one piece of wood so the grain matches when the drawer is closed. The flush drawer face fits neatly into the apron opening—also a trait of the Shaker style.

Construction details

Joinery. Trees just don't have the girth to yield slabs wide enough for tabletops and the like, but by butting together and edge-gluing two or more narrow boards you can create slabs as wide as you need. For our Shaker table, we edge-glued boards for the tabletop and the shelf. Edge-glued butt joints require square, smooth edges to ensure a good glue bond. A stationary power jointer is the best tool to joint edges. A hand-held jointer plane with a 24-in.-long sole is equally effective, but slower.

Face-gluing is a similar operation to edge-gluing. Sometimes called laminating, it's used to create thick stock from a few thinner pieces. We face-glued strips of maple together to form the stock from which we cut the legs for the table.

The Shakers and their furniture

The American Shaker sect, now extinct, was established in 1774 and flourished during the 19th century. The sect was distinguished by two particular practices. First, as the name suggests, Shakers would dance in unrestrained movements as they prayed. Second, the Shakers designed and built a body of furniture and household objects exalted for their simple beauty—an intentionally sharp contrast to the ornate Victorian furnishings of the day.

Kept alive in museums and books and through faithful reproductions, Shaker furniture is functional, without sacrificing aesthetics. It adapts easily to today's uses and blends in with both formal and informal decor. It also offers valuable lessons in design.

The trademark of the Shaker sect can be found on authentic Shaker-produced furniture.

The aprons are joined to the legs with mortise-and-tenon joints, a staple in any woodworker's joinery arsenal (See *illustration,* below left). We used dowel pins to reinforce the joints. In this project, you'll learn how to cut tenons with a shop-made tenoning jig and miter gauge (See *Mortise-and-tenon joints,* p. 48).

Tapering. The legs at the top of the valet table are 1¾ in. square, which is thick enough to cut the ⅞-in.-deep mortises that accept the ⅞-in.-long apron and rail tenons. The legs begin to taper just below the shelf, tapering to a thickness of 1 in. square at the bottoms.

Drawer joinery. The drawer for the valet table is a small five-sided box—two sides, a front, back and bottom. Small drawers can be glued and nailed together with butt joints. But to create a strong drawer that holds up to abuse, the drawer on our table is constructed just as the Shakers would do it, with a combination of grooves, dado joints, and rabbet-and-dado joints. The front edge of each drawer side is rabbeted and fits into a stopped dado plowed inside the drawer face. The dado is not cut all the way through the top of the face, so the joint remains concealed from the top when the drawer is open. The drawer back is recessed into dadoes cut into the drawer sides. The bottom fits into grooves cut into the drawer sides and face.

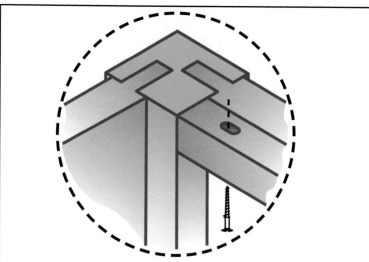

The mortises for the mortise-and-tenon joints used in this project are open on the top ends where they're cut into the legs of the table.

SHAKER TABLE

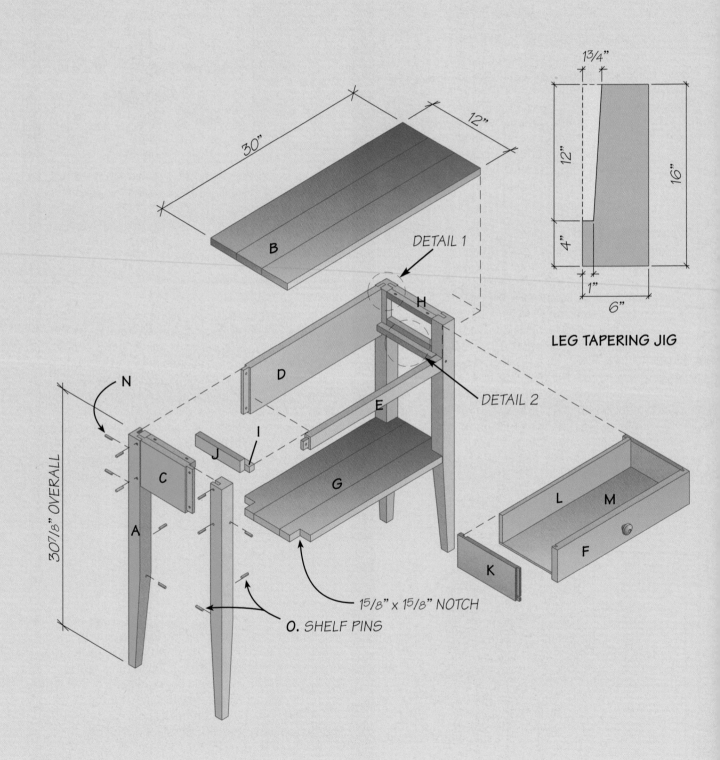

30"

12"

DETAIL 1

1³/4"

12"

16"

4"

1"

6"

LEG TAPERING JIG

B

H

DETAIL 2

N

D

E

I

J

C

G

L

M

A

K

F

30¹/8" OVERALL

1⁵/8" x 1⁵/8" NOTCH

O. SHELF PINS

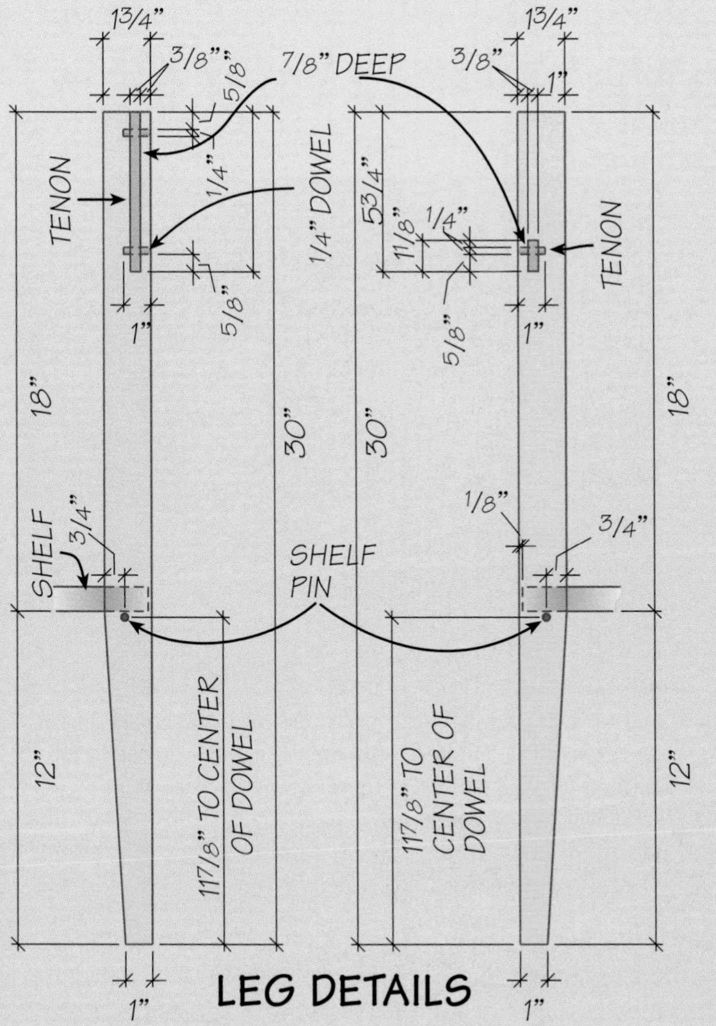

1 3/4"
3/8"
5/8"
7/8" DEEP
3/8"
1 3/4"
1"
TENON
1/4"
1/4" DOWEL
5 3/4"
1 1/8"
1/4"
TENON
1"
5/8"
5/8"
1"
18"
30"
30"
18"
1/8"
3/4"
SHELF
3/4
SHELF PIN
12"
11 7/8" TO CENTER OF DOWEL
11 7/8" TO CENTER OF DOWEL
12"
1"
1"

LEG DETAILS

FRONT LEG, INSIDE FACE

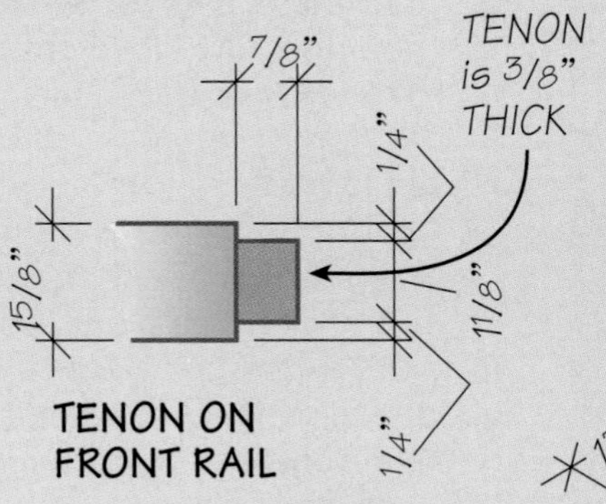

7/8"
TENON is 3/8" THICK
1/4"
1 5/8"
1 1/8"
1/4"

TENON ON FRONT RAIL

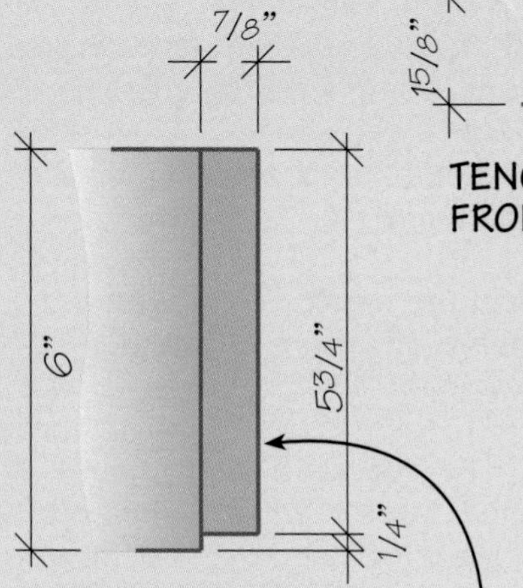

7/8"
6"
5 3/4"
1/4"

TENON ON SIDE & BACK APRONS

TENON is 3/8" THICK

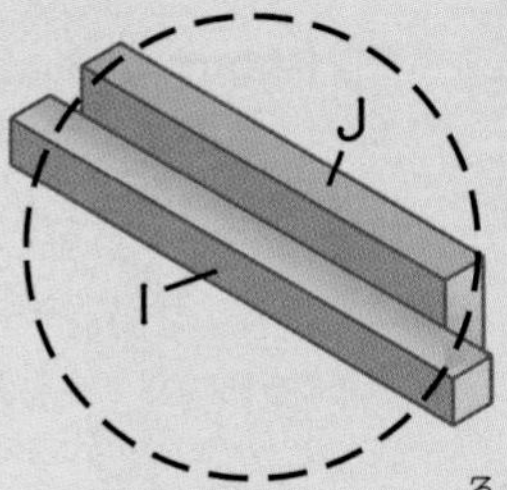

J
I

DETAIL 2: DRAWER GLIDE

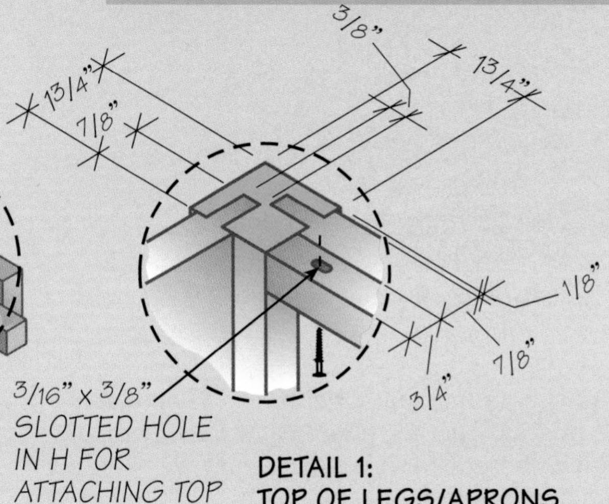

3/8"
1 3/4"
1 3/4"
7/8"
1/8"
7/8"
3/4"
3/16" x 3/8" SLOTTED HOLE IN H FOR ATTACHING TOP

DETAIL 1: TOP OF LEGS/APRONS, TOP CLEATS & TENONS

Shaker Table Cutting List

Part	No.	Size	Material
A. Legs	4	1¾ × 1¾ × 30″	Maple
B. Top	1	⅞ × 12 × 30″	"
C. Aprons (sides)	2	⅞ × 6 × 8¾″	"
D. Apron (back)	1	⅞ × 6 × 22¼″	"
E. Front Rail	1	⅞ × 1⅝ × 22¼″*	"
F. Drawer Face	1	⅞ × 4¼ × 20½″*	"
G. Shelf	1	⅞ × 10¼ × 23¾″	"
H. Top Cleats	2	¾ × ¾ × 7″	Pine
I. Drawer Glides	2	¾ × ¾ × 8½″	"
J. Drawer Guides	2	¾ × 1½ × 7″	"
K. Drawer Sides	2	½ × 4¼ × 8⅞″	"
L. Drawer Back	1	½ × 3⅝ × 20″	"
M. Drawer Bottom	1	¼″ × 8¼ × 20″	Lauan Plywood
N. Tenon Pins	14	¼″ dia. × 1″	Maple or Birch Dowel
O. Shelf Pins	8	¼″ dia. × 1″	Maple or Birch Dowel

*Cut drawer face and front rail from one 6″ wide board.

Project Assembly Steps: Shaker-style Valet Table

FIGURE B: The mortises in the tops of the legs should be laid out and cut before cutting the tapers. Use a marking gauge to lay out the cutting lines for the mortises (See *Cutting mortises,* page 48).

Glue-up the blanks for the parts

1 Select the boards for the tabletop and shelf. The total width of the boards when laid side to side should be at least ½ in. wider than the finished width of each part. If your boards are long enough, you can create one glued-up panel, then cross-cut both parts from it. If not, the boards should all be at least 1 in. longer than the finished length of the part. (See *Edge-gluing,* page 86).

2 Machine the boards. First, surface plane them so they all have smooth, even surfaces and are equal in thickness. Then, run the long edges across your jointer or hand plane them.

3 Wipe the mating edges clean, then arrange the boards so the cupping pattern of the grain alternates from board to board.

FIGURE A: Clamp the edge-glued boards together with pipe clamps or bar clamps and wood cauls (See *Edge-gluing,* page 86).

4 Apply glue to all mating surfaces, then clamp the boards together **(See FIGURE A).** NOTE: Edge-glued boards form a strong joint without any reinforcement, but if you can use biscuits or dowels to help keep the boards aligned. Alternate the clamps above and below the panels to equalize clamping pressure. Do not overtighten the clamps.

5 Select wood for the legs if you don't have any stock that's 2 in. square or bigger. Face-glue the pieces together (See *Face-gluing,* page 46).

6 Joint the blanks for the legs on one side, rip-cut them to width, then cut them to length. Do not taper the legs at this stage.

Make the legs

1 Lay out two ⅜-in-wide × ⅞-in.-deep × 5¾-in.-long mortises ⅜ in. in from adjacent faces at the top of each leg blank, using a marking gauge **(See FIGURE B)** or a pencil and square. Select one good face, without the laminations showing, as the outside front face of each leg.

2 Remove the waste in the mortise area with a drill press, then square off with a chisel (See *Mortise-and-tenon joints,* page 48).

3 Lay all the legs side by side, with the top and bottom edges aligned. Mark the lower shelf pin locations across each leg with a square 11⅞ in. up from the bottoms of the legs—this will ensure that all the pegs are the same height. Mark a centerpoint on each line an equal distance from each side, then bore ¼-in.-dia. × ¾-in.-deep dowel holes at each centerpoint.

4 Taper the legs using a tapering jig (See *Tapering jig,* page 47). Make sure the tapers are on the inside faces containing either a mortise or a dowel hole. Start the tapers 12 in. up from the leg bottoms. They should taper to 1 in. square at the bottoms.

Make the aprons

1 Rip-cut and cross-cut the side and back aprons to size. For practical reasons, cut the tenons on the front rail into the ends of a 1x6 workpiece used to make both the front rail and the drawer face. After you've cut the tenons, you'll need to rip-cut the workpiece to make the rail and drawer face, then cut the drawer face to length (See *Step 7*).

2 Lay out the shoulder and cheek cuts for ⅜-in.-thick × ⅞-in.-deep × 5¾-in.-long tenons on the side aprons, back apron and the drawer face/front rail workpiece, using a pencil and a square or a marking gauge. Make identical markings on a test piece the same thickness as the aprons.

3 Make a tenoning jig to guide the workpieces securely on-end through the saw blade (See *Tenoning jig,* page 50).

4 Set the table saw fence ⅜ in. from the blade and raise the blade to ⅞ in. above the table to cut the long tenon cheeks. Clamp the test piece to the tenon jig and make the first cheek cut, keeping the jig pressed securely against the fence. Flip the workpiece to make the second cheek cut. Check the thickness of the tenon area between test cuts. If it matches the width of the mortises in the legs, make cheek cuts on each apron. If it doesn't match, make adjustments as needed.

5 Set the saw fence ¼ in. from the blade. Make the short cheek cuts in the test piece by clamping it with the narrow edge against the tenoning jig (See *Tenoning jig,* page 50). Make the cuts on one end of the side aprons and the back apron.

6 Cut the tenon shoulders using the miter gauge and a scrap block clamped to the saw fence (See *Tenoning jig,* page 50). Adjust the setup until the resulting tenon fits snugly in the mortise, then make the shoulder cuts in all apron tenons.

FIGURE C: Glue and clamp the two side assemblies together. Wood cauls spanning between the clamp heads help distribute clamp pressure evenly. The side assemblies will be connected by the back apron and the front rail.

7 Draw a "V" across the drawer face/rail workpiece, then make a rip cut 1⅞ in. up from one long edge to separate the rail from the drawer face. Use the legs of the "V" as an alignment guide when positioning the parts later. Trim ¼ in. from the top and bottom edges of the tenons on the front rail, leaving tenons that are 1⅛ in. wide. Finally, cut the tenons off the drawer face so it's the right length to fit into the drawer opening.

Glue up the apron assembly

1 Assemble and glue the side aprons to the legs using two clamps and wood cauls at the joints **(See FIGURE C).** Make sure each apron assembly is square.

2 Glue the back apron and front rail to the side assemblies. Clamp the assembly using wood cauls until the glue dries.

3 Bore dowel holes for the tenon pins, then install them **(See**

FIGURE D: Reinforce the mortise-and-tenon joints with dowel pins.

FIGURE D) and cut them flush with the face of the leg (See *Pinned mortise-and-tenon joints,* page 52).

Build the drawer

1 Check the fit of the drawer face in the apron opening—there should be a gap no greater than 1/16 in. on each side and on the top. Plane or sand the edges of the drawer face, if needed. Use a router and straight bit to cut the 1/4-in.-wide × 3/8-in.-deep stopped dadoes in the insides of the drawer face (See *Dado-rabbet joints*, page 28). Stop the dadoes 1/4 in. from the top edges. These dadoes will accept rabbets in the drawer sides. Also cut a 1/4-in.-wide × 1/4-in.-deep groove on the inside of the drawer face, 3/8 in. up from the bottom, between the dado shoulders. This groove will accept the drawer bottom.

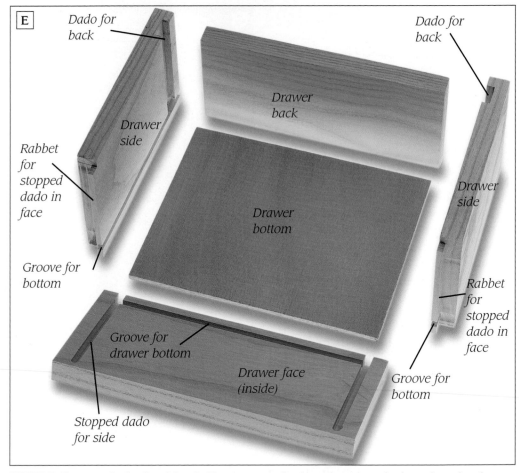

Dado for back

Dado for back

Drawer back

Drawer side

Rabbet for stopped dado in face

Drawer side

Groove for bottom

Drawer bottom

Rabbet for stopped dado in face

Groove for drawer bottom

Drawer face (inside)

Groove for bottom

Stopped dado for side

FIGURE E: The parts of a five-board, interlocking drawer are fitted together using only glue and a series of dadoes, grooves and rabbets (except the drawer bottom, which is attached using only wire brads).

2 Cut the drawer sides to size, then cut 1/4-in.-wide × 3/8-in.-deep drawer-bottom grooves in the sides, 3/8 in. up from the bottoms. Cut 3/8-in.-deep × 1/4-in.-thick rabbets in the ends of the drawer sides, then remove a 1/4-

FIGURE F: Glue the drawer frame together using bar clamps or pipe clamps and wood cauls. Make sure the corners are square.

in. section of the rabbet ledge at the top of each drawer side—these rabbets will fit into the stopped dadoes in the face **(See FIGURE E)**.

3 Rout 1/2-in.-wide dadoes in the drawer sides for the drawer back, starting 1/2 in. from the back edges of the sides. Stop the dadoes at the groove for the drawer bottom and square this intersection with a chisel.

4 Dry-assemble the sides and front and measure between the bottoms of the dadoes in the sides to get an accurate measurement for the drawer back. Make sure the sides are square to the front. Cut the back slightly shorter than the measured distance to leave room for glue in the joint. Dry-assemble the drawer. Measure for the drawer bottom. Cut the bottom, leaving very slight gaps (you should not glue the bottom panel in, but you want to make sure it slides easily into the grooves).

5 Glue and clamp the sides to the drawer front and back **(See FIGURE F)**. Make sure the top of the back is flush with the tops of the other parts. After the glue dries, insert the drawer bottom and check the drawer for square by measuring the diagonals. When square, attach the bottom by driving ¾-in. wire brads through the bottom panel and into the drawer back **(See FIGURE G)**.

Install the tabletop

1 Cut the tabletop to size from the glued-up blank, then smooth the top surface with a jack plane, planing first at a diagonal across the grain to clean the glue joints. Then, plane the top following the grain. Finish smoothing the tabletop with a cabinet scraper. NOTE: Using a belt sander is an effective and common method for smoothing and evening a glued-up panel, but it's messier and won't give you the same degree of smoothness.

2 Cut the top cleats to length. Because of expansion and contraction, we used slotted screw holes to attach the tabletop. That way, the screws can move laterally, but still retain their holding power. To make the slotted holes in the cleats, drill pairs of holes next to one another, then connect them with a chisel. Attach the cleats to the aprons with glue and screws.

3 Lay the tabletop upside-down and place the table on top of it. Orient the aprons with the tabletop for equal overhang on opposing sides. Mark the hole locations in the tabletop with an awl through the top-cleat screw holes **(See FIGURE H)**.

4 Remove the table base and bore pilot holes in the top at the awl marks; use a stop on your drill bit to avoid boring through the top. Attach the tabletop using screws with washers driven up through the top cleats.

Attach the drawer glides & guides

1 Cut the drawer glides and drawer guides to length. Join them with glue and screws so the bottoms of each pair are flush and the shorter guide is centered on the glide. Screw the assemblies to the side aprons so the glides are ¹⁄₁₆ in. above the front rail.

2 Test-fit the drawer. If the drawer face does not sit flush with the lower rail when closed, plane the back ends of sides with a block plane.

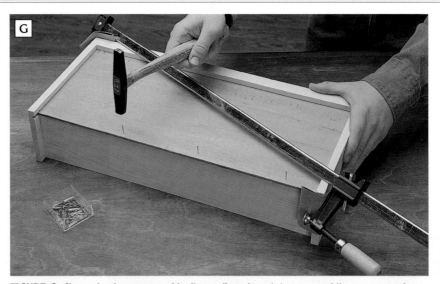

FIGURE G: Clamp the drawer assembly diagonally to keep it in square while you secure the plywood drawer bottom with wire brads (don't use glue).

FIGURE H: Attach the tabletop with screws, fitted with washers, driven through slotted holes in the cleats and into pilot holes in the tabletop.

Make the shelf

Cut the shelf to size from the glued-up panel. Cut a 1⅝ in. × 1⅝ in. notch at each corner. Drive 1-in.-long, ⅜-in.-dia. dowel pins into the dowel holes in the legs. Apply the finish and install the shelf.

Finishing touches

Install a wooden drawer pull, then finish sand all wood surfaces. Wipe clean and apply your finish of choice (See *Wood finishing*, page 54). Mount the shelf on top of the dowel pins in the legs.

Face-gluing

Face-gluing, sometimes called *laminating,* is the process of gluing up several strips of wood to make a thicker piece of stock (known as a *blank*). Because it's getting harder to find lumber that's more than 4/4 (1 in.) thick, face-gluing blanks is becoming an increasingly useful skill.

The overall thickness of the blank should be at least ⅛ in. thicker and 1 in. wider than required to allow for waste when you joint and trim the edges of the blank. Lay out the boards so the annual growth rings, visible on the end grain, cup in alternating directions. This will counteract the forces of the grain, preventing the assembly from cupping and delaminating. After the glue has dried completely, joint and trim the blank to the desired thickness.

HOW TO FACE-GLUE A LAMINATED BLANK

1 Plane both faces of each board until they're smooth and even, using a power planer or a hand plane. Plane in the same direction as the grain to avoid tearout. Remember that the final laminated blank should be about ⅛ in. thicker than needed. If you're using a power planer, be sure to let the rollers inside the tool draw the workpieces through the planer head—don't force them by hand.

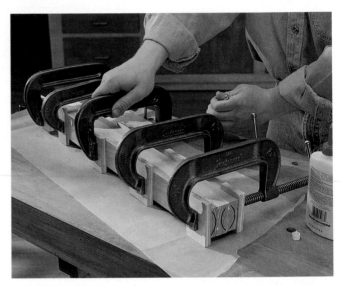

2 Arrange the boards so the end grain cups in alternating directions, then apply glue to each mating board face. Spread the glue evenly, then rub the boards together to create a suction effect. Clamp the glue-up, keeping the edges and ends aligned as well as you can (this can be tricky: wet glue acts as a lubricant and allows the pieces to shift). Use one clamp every 6 in. or so. Let the glue dry before unclamping.

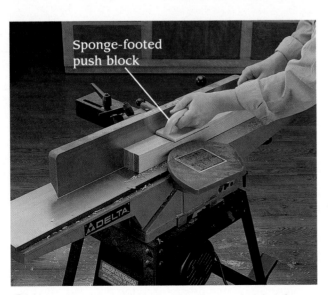

Sponge-footed push block

3 With the face of one of the outer boards pressed against the fence, run one laminated edge of the blank through the jointer until the surface is smooth and even all the way across.

4 Now that two adjacent sides are smooth and square, rip-cut the blank to finished size. Make sure the smooth faces ride against the fence and on the saw table. Use a push stick to guide the blank.

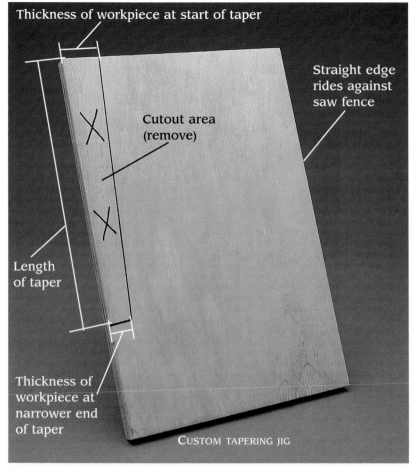

Thickness of workpiece at start of taper

Straight edge rides against saw fence

Cutout area (remove)

Length of taper

Thickness of workpiece at narrower end of taper

CUSTOM TAPERING JIG

A custom tapering jig made from plywood is easy to build, inexpensive, safe and virtually foolproof. A cutout in one corner of the plywood has the same dimensions and shape the non-waste area of the workpiece will have after the taper is cut. Once you remove the cutout with a jig saw, the workpiece is set into the pocket created by the cutout, then run through a table saw or band saw. (See photo below.)

Insert the workpiece into the cutout area of the jig and feed it through the blade to cut a perfect taper. Use a hold-down to keep the workpiece firmly against the table and the pocket in the jig. Use your hand or a push stick to push the jig and the workpiece forward.

Cutting tapers with a tapering jig

Taper cuts contribute an increased sense of style and craftsmanship to just about any woodworking project. But to cut them safely and accurately requires a tapering jig. There are many commercial tapering jigs and countless plans for shop-built adjustable tapering jigs available, but we've found that the simplest shop-built jig is often the best solution.

Making a plywood tapering jig

The tapering jig shown here can be used on a table saw or band saw. It begins with a rectangular piece of ¾-in. plywood. The size of the jig depends on the length of the taper. The longer the taper is, the longer the jig will need to be. The jig should be wide enough so there is plenty of material between the tapering area and the uncut edge that will ride against the fence of your saw.

Using the upper left corner of the plywood as a starting point, measure in along the top the thickness of the tapered workpiece at its thickest point. Then measure down the edge of the jig and mark the length of the taper. Measure in straight from that point and mark the thickness of the taper at its narrow end. Connect the point with a straightedge, and cut out along the outline with your jig saw.

Using the tapering jig

Set the saw fence so the uncut portion of the jig edge with the taper cutout just touches the saw blade when the opposite jig edge is pressed against the fence. With the jig well in front of the saw blade, position the workpiece inside the jig cutout. Turn on the saw and guide the jig and workpiece through the blade. Use your hand or a push stick to guide the jig, making sure it maintains contact with the fence. Use a hold-down to keep the workpiece pressed firmly against the table as you cut.

The mortise-and-tenon is one of the simplest and strongest wood joints. It's comprised of a narrow tenon carved in the end of one mating workpiece, which fits into a mortise hole in the other mating workpiece. The joint can simply be glued, or you can reinforce it with dowels or wedges.

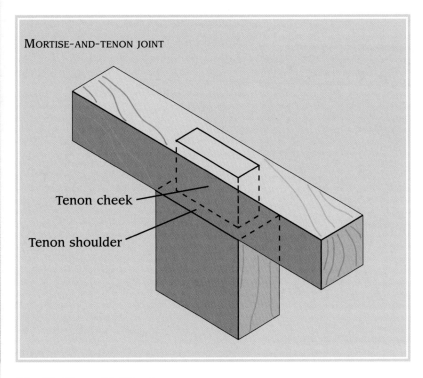

MORTISE-AND-TENON JOINT

Tenon cheek

Tenon shoulder

WOODWORKING SKILLS
Making mortise-and-tenon joints

The mortise-and-tenon joint is one of the strongest joint types for one simple reason: the fastener (the tenon) is actually part of the workpiece. In addition to their great strength, mortise-and-tenon joints are exceptionally versatile. Because you cut the parts of the joint yourself, you can give them just about any size or configuration you want. You can also reinforce them in any of a number of ways (if you want to reinforce them). Throughout this book, you'll find many variations of the basic mortise-and-tenon joint.

Cutting mortises

When making a mortise-and-tenon joint, it's best to begin by cutting the mortises first (after the workpieces are cut to size). In general, it's much easier to cut the tenon portion to fit the mortise—the range of thicknesses for cutting mortises is limited by the thickness of the workpiece and the diameters of the drill bits or router bits in your shop.

The most common method for cutting mortises is to use a drill or drill press to remove most of the waste in the mortise, then square the edges with a wood chisel. For shallow mortises, however, you can also use a router and straight bit (a plunge router is the better choice for this cut). If you expect to do a lot of mortising, look into buying a mortising attachment for your drill press. These attachments feature bit-type cutters housed in a sharpened sleeve that actually performs a chiseling action as you lower the spinning bit into the workpiece.

In general, you don't want to cut a mortise that's more than half the thickness of the workpiece. There should be at least ⅜ in. of wood between the edges of the mortise and the edge of the workpiece (except for mortises that begin at the top or bottom of a workpiece).

The best way to get consistent mortises is to perform each step in the operation on all workpieces before changing the tool set-up. And as with most joinery operations, make a test piece and check accuracy and dimensions before cutting actual workpieces.

HOW TO CUT A MORTISE BY DRILLING AND CHISELING

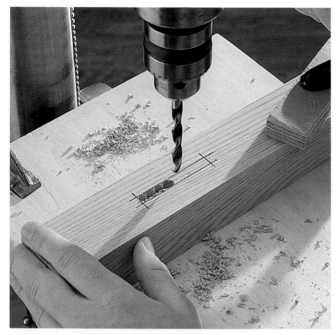

1 In your drill press, install a brad-point bit or Forstner bit with a diameter equal to the planned thickness of the mortise. Set the depth stop on the drill press to equal the depth of the mortise. Align the bit with the layout lines at one end of the mortise. To keep the bit aligned throughout, clamp a fence to the drill press table behind the workpiece. Bore one hole at a time. Once a hole is bored, move the workpiece so the next hole will be next to, or slightly overlapping, the first hole. Continue drilling until you reach the other end of the outline. Clamp the workpiece to the drill press table before drilling each hole.

2 Use sharp wood chisels to remove the remaining waste wood and clean the mortise walls. To avoid splitting the wood, start with a narrow chisel, equal to the width of the mortise, and square one end of the mortise. Keep the flat face of the chisel against the mortise wall as you work. Then use a wider chisel to clean out the length of the mortise. Let the chisel enter the mortise at an angle to help you control the cut, paring away the waste as you work. Finish the cut by chiseling straight up and down to clean the walls all the way to the mortise floor, or bottom. For square tenons, square off the ends of the mortises with a chisel. Some woodworkers prefer to round-over the ends of the tenons to fit the mortises.

HOW TO CUT MORTISES WITH A PLUNGE ROUTER

1 Lay out an outline for the mortise on the workpiece using a pencil and combination square. If you need to make mulitple mortises the same width and in alignment, use a marking gauge.

2 In your plunge router, install a straight bit with a diameter equal to the width of the mortise. Clamp a stop block guide to the router base so the bit aligns with the mortise outline. Set the cutting depth to the depth of the mortise. With the workpiece secured, plunge the bit into the wood and make the mortise cut.

Cutting tenons with a tenoning jig

The safest way to cut tenons on a table saw is with a tenoning jig. Variations on the jig abound. Some slide along the top of the saw fence or straddle it while others have a bar that fits into the miter slot. But the guiding principle should be the same for any jig: a safe tenoning jig should support the workpiece on one face and from behind, and act as a cradle to keep the workpiece secure as it passes through the saw blade. In addition, the jig should provide a means to clamp the workpiece so it resists the tendency to ride up over the blade or wander away from the fence. Clamping becomes more crucial the longer a tenon gets because more stock is being removed in a single pass, creating greater resistance on the blade.

The jig we show here can be made from two pieces of scrap stock screwed together at a right angle. It rides on top of the saw fence, which allows you to keep your hands at a safe distance from the blade and also provides additional vertical support for tall workpieces such as table aprons or face frame stiles. A contoured handle is cut at the rear of the jig for better gripping.

TENONING JIG
(FOR USE WITH TABLE SAW)

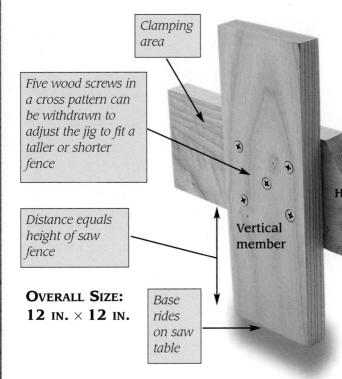

Clamping area

Five wood screws in a cross pattern can be withdrawn to adjust the jig to fit a taller or shorter fence

Distance equals height of saw fence

Vertical member

Handle

Horizontal member

OVERALL SIZE: 12 IN. × 12 IN.

Base rides on saw table

Bottom of horizontal member rides on saw fence

HOW TO CUT TENONS WITH A TENONING JIG

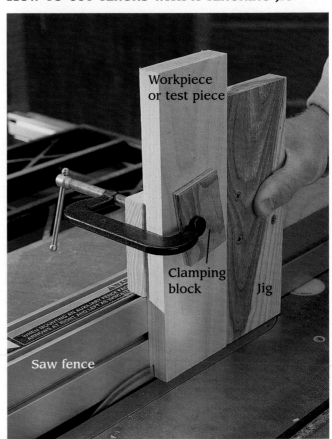

Workpiece or test piece

Clamping block

Jig

Saw fence

1 Make the cheek cuts first (parallel to the wood grain). Clamp the workpiece to the jig so it's snug against the face of the vertical support and the front edge of the horizontal support, resting flat on the saw table. Set the saw fence so the distance to the opposite face of the blade equals the amount of waste being removed, and raise the blade to equal the depth of the tenon. Rest the jig on the fence and feed the workpiece through the blade to make the cut. Flip the workpiece, reclamp, and make the cheek cut on the other face (for centered tenons). Always make cuts on a test piece first, and check the dimensions for accuracy.

This shop-made tenoning jig rides on the saw fence, giving support to workpieces set on-end as they pass through the blade. The vertical member extends down to the saw table and serves to square the workpiece to the blade and to support it from the rear. It's very important that the distance from the bottom of the horizontal member to the bottom of the vertical member be exactly the same as the height of your table saw fence.

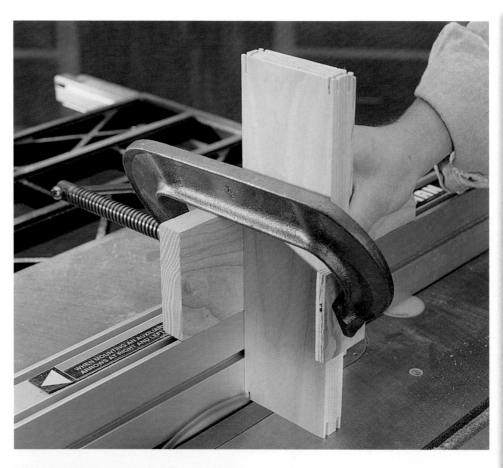

2 For notched tenons that don't run the full width of the workpiece, make additional cheek cuts on the short edges of the workpiece. Clamp the workpiece at a right angle to the jig, with the edge flat against the horizontal member and the face of the workpiece pressed against the front edge of the vertical member. Reset the saw fence if the amount of waste being removed is different than with the first cheek cuts. Make sure that everything is held securely in place, and guide the jig and workpiece through the blade. Flip and reclamp the workpiece to cut the other short cheek.

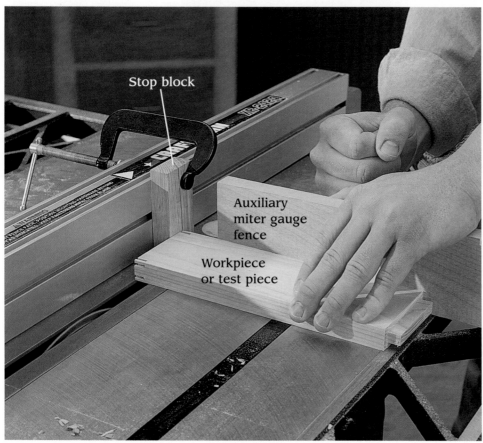

Stop block

Auxiliary miter gauge fence

Workpiece or test piece

3 Make the shoulder cuts (across the grain of the workpiece) using a miter gauge as a guide. For stability, we attached an auxiliary wood fence to the miter gauge. Also clamp a stop block to the table saw fence for use as an alignment guide and to keep the workpiece from binding against the fence and allows the waste to fall away freely rather than getting trapped between the fence. Adjust the fence so the workpiece, when butted against the block, can slide forward on the miter gauge and meet the blade at the base of the tenon cheek. Raise the blade above the table high enough to cut the shoulders without scoring the tenon. Cut the shoulders on each face, then reset the blade height if necessary, and cut shoulders on the ends of the tenon.

Pinning mortise-and-tenon joints

Mortise-and-tenon joints are inherently strong, but for a little extra reinforcement they can be pinned with through dowels. A pinned mortise-and-tenon joint is ideal for high-stress joints, like those found where vertical and horizontal furniture members are joined.

There are two basic methods for constructing a pinned (sometimes called *pegged*) mortise-and-tenon joint. One is to bore a hole through the tenon and another through the mortise before the joint is assembled. If you offset these holes slightly, the joint will be drawn together tightly when the dowel is driven through it (See *Offset dowel pins,* page 69). A more common method is simply to drill a dowel hole through the joint after it is glued and assembled, as shown here. This type of pinning doesn't contribute greatly to the strength of the joint, but it does provide a valuable back-up in the event that the glue joint fails.

The exposed ends of dowels provide a nice decorative detail, especially when they're oriented so the grain runs in the opposite direction of the board the dowel is set into.

1 Cut the mortises and tenons, then glue and clamp the joint (See Tenoning jig, page 50 and Cutting mortises, page 48). Let the glue set up, then lay out the location of the pins with a pencil and combination square. Use at least two evenly spaced pins for each joint, making sure the guide holes are at least ⅜ in. from the edges of the boards.

PINNED MORTISE AND TENON
JOINT ILLUSTRATION

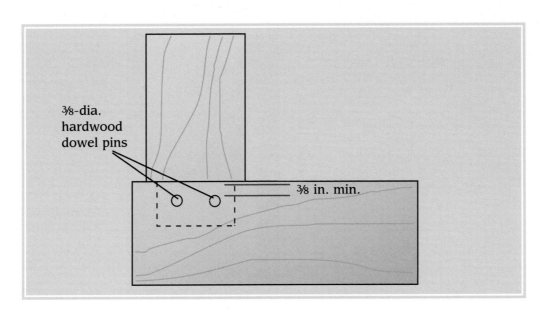

⅜-dia. hardwood dowel pins

⅜ in. min.

Pinned mortise-and-tenon joints

2 Punch a small starter hole at the centerpoint of each pin hole. If your project is a manageable size, use your drill press to drill the holes, as we did in the photo above. Using a brad-point bit will ensure that the hole starts precisely in the centerpoint. Drill the holes all the way through the tenon and into the other side of the mortise. Use a bit stop if your plan calls for stopped pins. If you're creating through-pin joints, drill all the way through the joint and into a piece of scrap.

3 Cut the pins from hardwood dowels, normally of the same species as the workpieces. TIP: For a decorative touch, use dowels made of wood with a naturally contrasting wood tone (for example, maple pins driven into walnut workpieces). Taper the lead tip of the dowel slightly so it will enter the hole more easily. Squeeze a little glue into each hole, then tap the dowel pins home with a wood mallet. Stop tapping when the dowel seats at the bottom of the hole.

4 Trim the dowels flush with the leg surface—here we use a flexible, fine-tooth Japanese-style saw. Depending upon the amount of dowel you need to remove, you may be able to smooth the ends flush with a file instead of sawing them off.

5 Finally, remove any excess glue with a scraper and sand the surface smooth with sandpaper and a wooden sanding block.

Shaker-style Valet Table   53

WOODWORKING SKILLS
Applying a wood finish

A well-chosen and well-applied finish is the final (and one of the most critical) steps in any woodworking project. As you gain experience finishing, you'll undoubtedly discover some favorite finishing products—and there are a dizzying number to choose from.

Basically, a wood finish has from two to four primary components. Some types of wood (especially softwoods) take stain more evenly if you apply a coat of wood conditioner first. Another option is paste filler or grain filler, which is used frequently on open-pore woods like oak. If you want to darken the tone of the wood or highlight a grain pattern, apply a coloring agent (wood dye or stain). Finally, apply a clear, protective topcoat such as tung oil or varnish.

Tack cloths: A fine-finish essential

Pre-made tack cloth

Ingredients for shop-made tack cloths

Tack cloth options. Tack cloths are sold premade and prepackaged at most woodworking stores. You can also make your own by blending small amounts of boiled linseed oil and varnish, then coating a piece of cheese cloth with the mixture. Store tack cloths in a sealed jar.

A perfectly clean wood surface is critical to successfully applying wood finishing products. Even tiny amounts of dust can ruin an otherwise perfect finish. The best way to thoroughly clean a wood surface before applying a finish is to wipe it with a tack cloth. Tack cloths draw fine particles up out of the pores of the wood without leaving any residue behind.

HOW TO APPLY A WOOD FINISH

1 After filling nail holes and wood defects with stainable wood putty, sand all surfaces with progressively finer paper, beginning with 150-grit. Work up to 180-grit, then finally 220-grit for most wood species. A random-orbit sander is excellent for flat surfaces. TIP: Before you apply the stain, wipe the workpiece with a clean, water-dampened sponge to check for dried glue. Dried glue will appear as a clear glossy patch. Scrape away any glue with a cabinet scraper, then lightly sand again with 220-grit paper after the wood dries.

2 Remove sawdust with a soft-bristled brush or by blowing with compressed air. Then, use a tack cloth to give the wood surfaces a thorough cleaning. Even if you're working in a dedicated clean room for finishing, wipe the surfaces with a tack cloth again if you wait more than a few minutes before applying the finishing products.

3 Wearing rubber gloves, apply wood stain (if you choose to use it) with a clean, lint-free cloth. Cover the entire project part (for example, the tabletop) completely. Follow the application instructions on the product container. For best results, apply a thin coat.

4 Allow the stain to penetrate into the wood for a few moments (see the instructions on the container), then wipe away any excess product. For a darker wood tone, repeat the application procedure. NOTE: Topcoats applied over stain normally darken the finish. To get an accurate idea of what tone the topcoated wood will have, evaluate the finish while the stain is still wet.

5 Let the stained workpiece dry overnight, then apply the first coat of topcoating material. Whether you're using a brush, a wiping rag or even a sprayer, the coat should be very thin to prevent sagging as the product dries. Avoid overworking the topcoat with your brush. Generally, thinning the topcoat product slightly is a good idea for the first coat.

6 When the first coat is dry, sand lightly by hand with 400-grit sandpaper to smooth out wood grain that may have been raised by the moisture in the product (especially if using a water-based product). Wipe with a tack cloth, then apply a second coat of undiluted finish material. Repeat the procedure. Most topcoat materials should be applied in at least three coats.

Mission-style Side Chair

As a stand-alone utility chair or part of a dining room set, this classic side chair is sure to find a space in your home. Made of solid red oak, the straightforward design is based on the popular Mission style. Comfortable and built to last, this chair can be adapted to fit just about any home decor when you select matching upholstery and finishing materials.

Woodworking Skills You'll Learn:

- Basics of chair design

- Chamfering with a disc sander

- Making repetitive cross-cuts

- Using strap clamps

- Making seat blocks

- Using offset pins to secure a mortise-and-tenon joint

- Making a cushioned chair seat

- Making a slatted backrest

- Resawing lumber on your band saw

Design Features

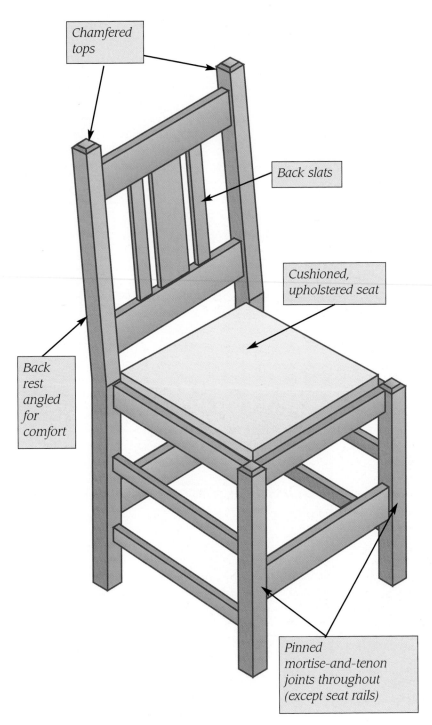

Chamfered tops

Back slats

Cushioned, upholstered seat

Back rest angled for comfort

Pinned mortise-and-tenon joints throughout (except seat rails)

**OVERALL SIZE:
38 IN. HIGH BY 17 IN. WIDE BY 17 IN. DEEP**

Mission-style Side Chair

Side chairs are usually associated with dining room sets, where their efficient proportions allow as many diners as possible to slide up to the dinner table. The chair shown in this project section certainly could be reproduced in multiple numbers to create a stylish and sturdy set of dining chairs. But it can also provide excellent service as a lone addition to just about any room in the house: next to the telephone at a desk, near an entryway, or anywhere that seating is desired but space is limited.

This oak side chair is designed in the tradition of Mission-style furniture, one of the most popular furniture styles today. With their square lines, prominent oak surfaces and trademark mortise-and-tenon joinery, Mission-style home furnishings are exceptionally adaptable to just about any environment and decorating scheme.

General planning

The style and proportions are the first issues to address when designing a chair. Because side chairs fall into a fairly limited range of sizes (See page 59), the main difference between models are in the proportions of the seat and backrest to one another, and in the wood type and extensiveness of ornamentation.

Parts of a side chair. A chair is essentially a frame made up of four legs connected by a series of horizontal rails and supporting a seat and backrest. The *legs* provide vertical support. Frequently, the rear and front legs are radically different in scale, if not design. In the chair shown here, the rear legs actually extend up past the seat area, then taper back to become the primary support for the backrest. Both the front and rear legs feature tops chamfered on all sides to remove any sharp edges and add style. The *seat* is made of a plywood seatboard that supports an upholstered foam cushion. The seatboard is attached to four *seat blocks* that fit into the corners formed by the four *seat rails*, which create a frame just below the tops of the front legs. Additional *rails* beneath the seat rails form an open box with the

Wood milling options

Quartersawn red oak

Plain (face) sawn red oak

Quartersawn lumber (top) is generally pre-ferred over the more common and less costly plain sawn (also called face-sawn) lumber (below). Quartersawn boards tend to be more stable and have better grain figure.

About red oak

Red oak can be found practi-cally anywhere you look in woodworking and finish car-pentry. Strong and relatively inexpensive, it's ideal for larger woodworking pro-jects that require highly fig-ured hardwood, as well as for interior moldings, hardwood floors, and other types of millwork. Its light-red color when finished creates a sense of warmth, but is gener-ally thought to be less desirable than the light golden glow of the other oak: white oak (See *About white oak,* page 117).

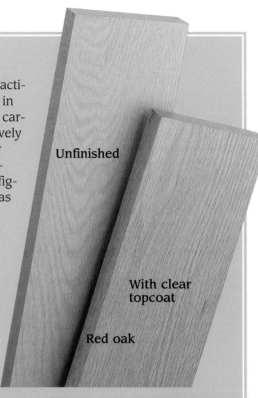

Unfinished

With clear topcoat

Red oak

Grain: Red oak has a straight grain with a coarse texture. The wood pores are open and noticeable. Better boards display *rays* that run perpendicular to the grain pattern for a pleasing effect.
Workability: The straight grain is relatively easy to work with hand and power tools, although the coarse texture can blunt cutters.
Finishing: The large pores cause stains to be splotchy. To obtain a more even finish, fill the wood pores with a paste (grain) filler, or use a gel stain before applying a finish.

legs, providing strength and lateral sup-port. The *backrest* is formed by a pair of rails that sandwich tenoned vertical slats.

Dimensions. The two most important dimensions are *seat height* and *seat depth.* Factors that determine these dimensions are the relative size of the people who will be using the chair or chairs (have your family members test several chairs for comfort), and the size and scale of any table or desk you plan to use the chair with (See *Design specs,* right). For a side chair, the seat is typically 16 to 18 in. high, 14 to 18 in. deep, and 16 to 20 in. wide. The seat on this chair is 18 in. high and 15 in. square, which is somewhat on the small side, but not problematic since the chair has no arms. On many chairs, but not normally side chairs, the seat slopes down from front to back at about a 5° angle. The size and angle of the backrest also are important to chair com-fort. The upper portions of the back legs taper back at a slight angle to increase comfort. Typically, a backrest should slant back at a 10° to 15° angle. The top of the back for a side chair should be 38 to 48 in. from the floor.

Design specs

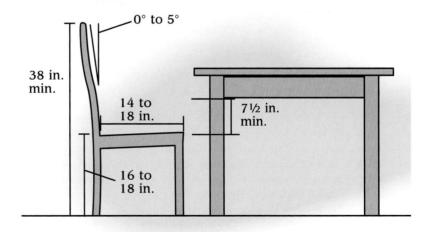

0° to 5°

38 in. min.

14 to 18 in.

7½ in. min.

16 to 18 in.

Side chair dimensions should take into account the comfort of the chair, as well as the proportions of any table or desk for which it's intended.

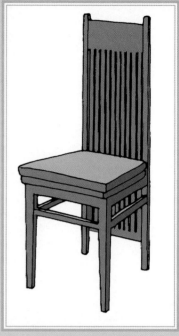

This bow-back chair is a variation of the popular Windsor chair style. Building one requires a considerable amount of wood bending and spindle turning on the lathe.

A typical oak side chair with caned seat from the turn of the century, this style features a pressed back and spindle-turned rails. Making this type of chair requires scooping or contouring the backrest.

In addition to his architectural accomplishments, Frank Lloyd Wright was a prominent furniture designer. The chair above is typical of his style, with the slatted, symmetrical oak panel in back.

Selecting upholstery

Solids   Prints

Selecting the right upholstery for your project is as important to the final appearance as selecting the right wood. Because chairs tend to take a good deal of abuse and are prone to spillage, look for sturdy fabric that's easy to clean. Treating the fabric with a spray-on protectant is usually a good idea. The design and color of the fabric falls into two basic categories: solids and prints. Leather and leather-look fabrics (very common on MIssion-style furniture) are normally solid in tone.

Material. Reproduction Mission-style furnishings being built today are normally made from quartersawn oak, although the originals were often made from cherry as well. Quarter sawing is a more expensive method of milling than plain (face) sawing. Quartersawn logs are cut radially to the growth rings and yield fewer boards than plain-sawn logs, which are cut tangentially. But quartersawn boards are considered more appealing by most furnituremakers because they often reveal the decorative rays found in oak. The rays reflect more light than the rest of the board and stand out when the wood is finished. You can tell if lumber is quarter-sawn by looking at the growth rings on the end grain: The growth rings run perpendicular to the wide board face. The growth rings on plain-sawn lumber run parallel with the board's face. Because of economy, availability, and the fact that it wasn't our goal to create an exact reproduction of a Mission piece, we used plain-sawn oak for our chair (although if you look closely you can see that a few of the parts appear to be quartersawn oak). For the same reasons, we also chose red oak over white oak—a more common wood for furniture of this style.

Aesthetics. The look and style of this side chair were mostly predetermined by the Mission style the design is based upon: strong lines and plenty of wood surface being the dominant themes. The seat upholstery was the main variable—we chose an American Southwest patterned material.

The Art-and-Crafts arm chair is closely related to the Mission furniture, with its strong rectilinear lines, oak construction and heavy use of mortise-and-tenon joinery. As with Mission chairs, most were upholstered in leather.

Similar to the Mission-style side chair described in this chapter, this version has a slightly different seat construction and features a leather upholstered backrest.

Construction details

Many modern chairs are constructed with doweled frames. Doweling a chair's front, back, side and seat rails to the legs makes it fairly easy to build. But when it comes to imparting structural integrity to a chair, doweled joints are second best. Instead, we used pinned mortise-and-tenon joints that yield a long-lasting joint and are true to the joinery used by the better craftsmen of Mission furniture. Each mortise-and-tenon joint is designed to suit the thickness of the wood being joined, so not all mortise-and-tenons are the same. Carefully note the mortise-and-tenon dimensions in the chair drawings before you cut them.

The back slats for the chair were made by resawing oak boards into ½-in.-thick strips on a bandsaw. The back legs are cut from laminated 5½-in.-wide stock, following a pattern.

Finishing. Mission furniture was not stained but rather colored by fuming the oak with ammonia in an airtight container. Before fuming, the pores were filled with a mixture of turpentine, raw linseed oil, and thickener. Once fumed, the furniture was coated with black wax. Today, there's little advantage to this method—unless you want to match existing pieces of original Mission furniture. We used paste (grain) filler to fill the open red oak pores, then applied a light-oak stain followed by two coats of polyurethane varnish.

MORTISE-AND-TENON JOINT (PINNED)

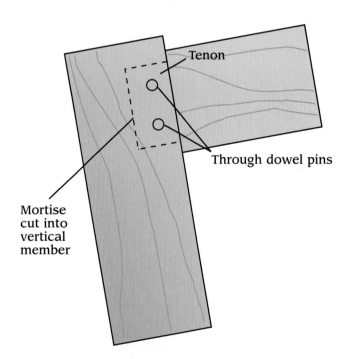

The mortise-and-tenon joint is a hallmark of Mission-style furniture. The joint shown above is a pinned mortise-and-tenon, with the tenon stopping midway through the mortised member. Through-mortises with exposed end-grain on the tenons were also used frequently in this style.

MISSION CHAIR

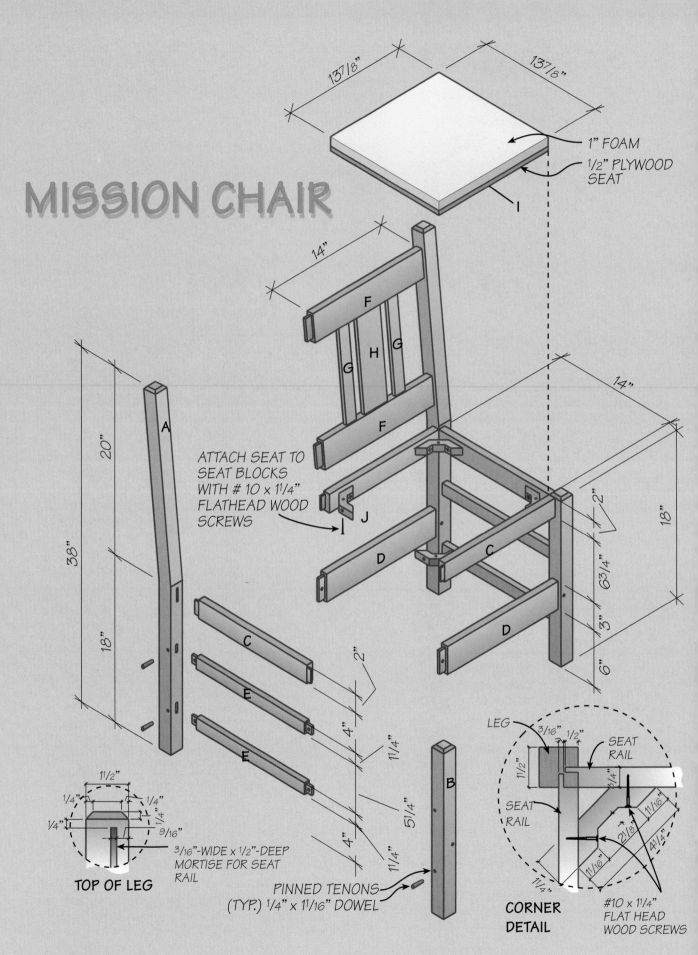

13⅞"

13⅞"

1" FOAM

½" PLYWOOD SEAT

I

14"

F

G H G

G

F

14"

2"

18"

6¾"

3"

6"

20"

38"

18"

ATTACH SEAT TO SEAT BLOCKS WITH # 10 x 1¼" FLATHEAD WOOD SCREWS

A

J

C

D

C

D

C

E

E

2"

4"

4"

1¼"

5¼"

4"

1¼"

B

TOP OF LEG

1½"

¼"

¼"

¼"

¼"

9/16"

3/16"-WIDE x ½"-DEEP MORTISE FOR SEAT RAIL

PINNED TENONS (TYP.) ¼" x 1¹/₁₆" DOWEL

LEG

3/16"   ½"

SEAT RAIL

1½"

¾"

SEAT RAIL

2⅛"

1¹/₁₆"

1¹/₁₆"

4¼"

1¹/₁₆"

¼"

CORNER DETAIL

#10 x 1¼" FLAT HEAD WOOD SCREWS

Mission Chair Cutting List

Part	No.	Size	Material		Part	No.	Size	Material
A. Rear legs	2	1½ × 1½ × 38"*	Red Oak		**F.** Upper Back Rails	2	¾ × 3 × 15½"	Red Oak
B. Front legs	2	1½ × 1½ × 18"	"		**G.** Back Slats	2	⅜ × 1¼ × 10¾"	"
C. Seat Rails	4	¾ × 2 × 15"	"		**H.** Back Slat	1	⅜ × 3 × 10¾"	"
D. Lower Front/ Back Rails	2	¾ × 3 × 15½"	"		**I.** Seat	1	½ × 13⅞ × 13⅞"	Plywood
E. Lower Side Rails	4	⅝ × 1¼ × 15½"	"		**J.** Seat Blocks	4	¾ × 1¼ × 4¼"	Hardwood

*Cut both from 1½ × 5½ × 38" piece

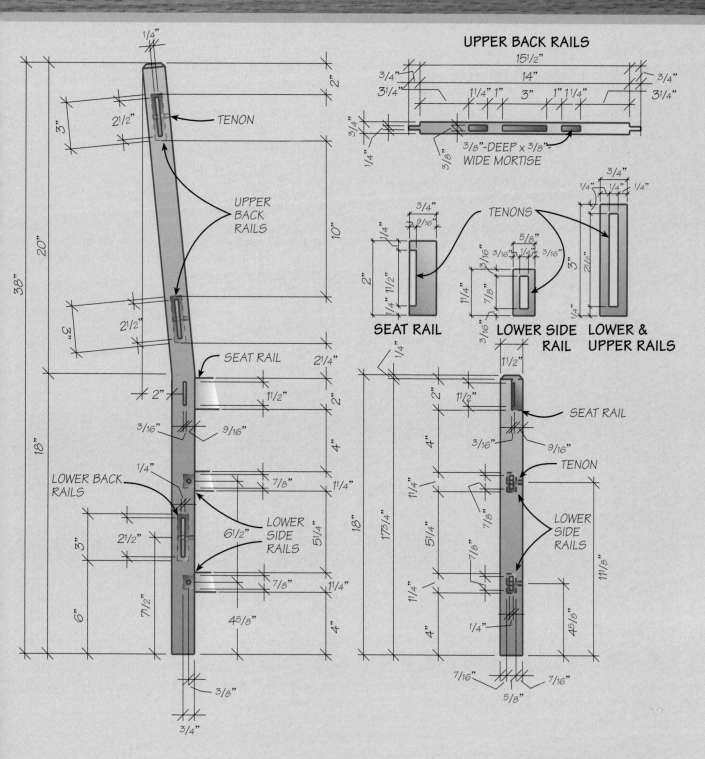

Project Assembly Steps: Mission-style Side Chair

Make the legs

1 Start by making the 1½-in.-square stock for the legs either by thickness planing 8/4 (2 in.) stock or face-gluing thinner stock (See *Face-gluing*, page 46). You can cut both rear legs from one 1½-in.-thick × 5½-in.-wide piece. Square the leg stock on a jointer. Rip-cut the stock for the front legs to width (1½ in. square). Rip-cut the back legs to 1½ in. thick (the width should remain 5½ in.), then cut the workpieces to length (38 in.).

2 Make a template pattern for the back legs or lay out the leg angles directly onto the workpieces (See *back leg detail*, page 63, and *Templates*, page 29).

3 Make the cut for the straight part of the leg on a table saw or band saw using a fence. If working on a table saw, remove the saw's anti-kickback pawls—once you complete the straight part of the cut, hold the workpiece in place and shut off the saw. Cut the angled portions of the back legs with a band saw or jig saw, then remove the saw marks with a smoothing rasp and cabinet scraper (or a random-orbit sander). To ensure the profiles are identical, you can gang-sand them by clamping them together and using an orbital sander to smooth the surfaces **(See FIGURE A).**

4 Cut the front legs to length on a radial arm saw or on a table saw with a miter gauge. Use a stop block as a guide to make sure the legs are the same length (18 in.).

5 Lay out the mortises on the inside faces of the front legs according to the dimensions in the plan drawing (page 63). Lay out the mortises in the rear legs as well. Measure carefully so the layout lines on opposite legs align. Cut the mortises (See *Cutting mortises*, page 48).

FIGURE A: Gang-sand the profiles on the back legs to ensure that they are identical. A random-orbit sander is a good tool choice.

FIGURE B: Dry-fit all the chair parts to assemble the chair frame and test the fit.

6 Chamfer the tops of the legs to remove the sharp edges. We used a benchtop disc/belt sander to grind the chamfers (See *Chamfering,* page 72). You could also use a block plane or a chamfering bit in a router.

Make the rails

1 On your bandsaw, resaw stock to ⅝ in. thick to make the four lower side rails (See *Resawing,* page 70). If you don't have access to a bandsaw, you can surface plane ¾-in.-thick stock to the correct thickness. Make sure you have some extra stock to use for test pieces. The seat rails and upper back rails can be made from premilled ¾-in. stock, or planed 4/4 lumber.

2 Rip-cut the lower side rails to width on your band saw or table saw. Cross-cut them to length on your power miter box or radial arm saw. Use a stop block to speed up the cutting and to ensure that the opposite rails are of equal length (See *Repetitive cuts,* page 68).

3 Cut ¼-in.-thick × ⅞-in.-wide × ¾-in.-deep tenons on the ends of the lower side rails, using a tenoning jig (See *Tenoning jig,* pages 50 to 51).

4 Cut ³⁄₁₆-in-thick × ½-in.-deep tenons on the ends of the seat rails by making a ½- × ⁹⁄₁₆-in. rabbet cut in each end (to allow the tenons to extend as far forward into the legs as possible). Make these cuts in two passes on a table saw with a tenoning jig: one vertical cut for the cheek, a second to expose the shoulder.

5 Cut ¼-in.-thick × 2½-in.-wide × ¾-in.-deep tenons on the ends of the lower front rail, lower back rail and both upper back rails, using a table saw and tenoning jig.

Make the back slats

1 Resaw or plane stock to ⅜ in. thick for the three back slats. Rip-cut the stock to 1¼ in. wide for the two narrow outer slats, and 3 in. for the center slat. Cross-cut the slats to length (10¾ in.). The slats are not to be tenoned.

2 Lay out and cut the ⅜-in.-deep × ⅜-in.-wide mortises for the back slats in the facing edges of the upper back rails (See *Cutting mortises,* page 48). The length of each mortise should equal the width of the back slats. Space them 1 in. apart, according to the *Diagram* on page 63.

FIGURE C: Driving a wood dowel pin through the offset dowel holes in the mortise and the tenon draws the joint together securely.

Assemble the chair frame

1 Dry-fit the back slats into the upper back rails **(See FIGURE B)**, then fit the upper back rail tenons into the upper mortises in the back legs. Insert seat rails and the lower front rails into the front legs, then connect the front and back leg assemblies by dry-fitting the lower side rails and seat rails between them. Make sure all joints are tight and square. Make any needed adjustments.

2 Disassemble the chair frame so you can drill the guide holes for the offset pins used to draw the joints together (See *Offset dowel pins,* page 69). Lay out and bore a guide hole for the dowel peg through the center of each mortise except the seat rail mortises.

3 Mark and bore a dowel guide hole in each mating tenon. The hole should be offset very slightly in the direction of the tenon shoulder. This slight offset will cause the joint to pull together tightly when the joint is glued and assembled.

4 Reassemble the chair frame in the same sequence as when dry-fitting. Apply glue to each mating surface (except the back slats), and drive dowel pins into the offset dowel holes as you assemble each individual joint **(See FIGURE C)**. If the pins protrude above the surface, cut them flush with the wood surface, using a tenon saw.

5 Check the joints for square and adjust as needed. Clamps should not be necessary when assembling, but can be used if the joints do not pull together all the way, or for a little added insurance **(See FIGURE D)**.

FIGURE D: Pinning the mortise-and-tenon joints with offset dowels virtually eliminates the need for clamps, but you may want to wrap a strap clamp around the seat frame just to be on the safe side.

Make the seat blocks & seat

1 Cut the seat blocks **(See FIGURE F)** from ¾-in.-thick hardwood, according to the diagram on page 62. Use a band saw or jig saw to cut the screw access notches. Make one block for each corner. Glue and screw the seat blocks into the inside corners of the seat-rail rail frame, ½ in. down from the tops of the seat rails.

2 Cut the square seatboard from ½-in. plywood. Laminated plywood is better for this purpose than solid core or medium-density fiberboard (MDF) plywood.

3 Cut the 1-in.-thick foam seat cushion and your chosen upholstery (See *Upholstering*, page 73). Wrap and attach the materials to the seat board. (*Tip: A layer of thin cloth between the foam and the upholstery makes the cushion more stable.*)

Finishing touches

Fill, sand and finish the wood (See pages 54 to 55). We used light oak stain and two coats of polyurethane. Screw the seat to the seat blocks from beneath, using #10 × 1¼-in. wood screws **(See FIGURE E)**.

FIGURE E: Drive #10 × 1¼-in. wood screws through countersunk pilot holes in the seat blocks to attach the cushioned seatboard to the chair frame.

F

1¼ in.

4 in.

Seat blocks cut from ¾-in. hardwood are attached at the inside corners of the seat frame to provide support for the seat, as well as a means for attaching it. The notch in the center allows you to drive screws squarely into the inside faces of the seat rails.

WOODWORKING SKILLS
Using pushsticks & featherboards

Hands and saw blades don't mix. As a safety precaution, use pushsticks and featherboards to guide and secure your work whenever possible. Using these simple devices may seem like an annoyance, but you'll quickly get used to them. Most experienced and professional woodworkers own vast collections of shop-made pushsticks and featherboards, and wouldn't even consider working without them.

Pushsticks typically have a handle and a back lip that "grips" the workpiece. In some cases, the safest way to use a pushstick is to run it through the blade, along with the workpiece (we don't suggest that you use fine hardwood for making these tools). Featherboards are slotted pieces of scrap wood that you clamp to the saw table or fence. They help keep the workpiece stable as it runs past them, and they also help prevent kickback.

Because the table saw is one of the few power saws where you move the workpiece into the blade (as opposed to taking the blade to the workpiece) many pushsticks and featherboards are designed for use with this common shop tool.

Pushsticks and featherboards let you keep your hands away from the saw blade, and help to stabilize the workpiece as it is being cut. In the photo above, a featherboard clamped to the saw fence prevents the workpiece from chattering or even kicking out of the saw. Another featherboard is clamped to the saw table to maintain consistent pressure against the saw fence. A simple pushstick is being used to feed the workpiece into the blade.

Make an assortment of pushsticks and featherboards for various cutting operations. Shown above (clockwise from bottom) are: a pushstick for rip-cutting; a commercial hold-down clamp that fits into the miter gauge slot; a long-handled pushstick for use with a featherboard; a closed-handle pushstick for cutting dadoes and rabbets; a featherboard clamped to the saw fence.

A pushstick, featherboard and hold-down are used in conjunction with the blade guard and a roller-type work support for a safe demonstration of rip-cutting on the table saw.

WOODWORKING SKILLS
Making repetitive cuts

Setting up to make repetitive cuts has two primary benefits: it's much faster than measuring and marking each workpiece individually, and it ensures that all the workpieces will be of uniform length.

You can make repetitive cuts on most stationary saws by clamping a stop block to the saw fence. Use the stop block as a guide for properly positioning the workpiece relative to the saw blade. With a table saw, the block is set on the infeed side of the blade, well back from it (See *photo, right*), and is used to set the position of the workpiece against the miter gauge. Then the workpiece is fed into the saw with the miter gauge. On radial arm saws and power miter boxes, the block is clamped to the fence for positioning the workpiece, which remains stationary as the blade cuts (See *photos* below).

To prevent sawdust from accumulating between the stop block and the workpiece, which could affect your cuts, cut a notch in the end of the stop block.

HOW TO MAKE REPETITIVE CUTS WITH A TABLE SAW

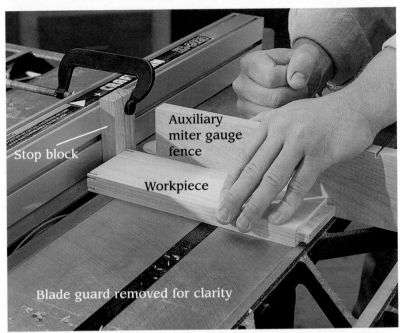

To make repetitive cuts on a table saw, clamp a stop block on the blade side of the fence so the distance from the block to the blade is equal to the amount you want to cut off each workpiece. Make sure the stop block is well back from the blade. With an auxiliary fence attached to your miter gauge, position the workpiece against the miter gauge fence so it's just touching the stop block, then press it firmly against the fence as you pass it through the saw blade.

HOW TO MAKE REPETITIVE CUTS WITH A RADIAL ARM SAW

1 Clamp a piece of scrap wood to the radial arm saw fence. The distance from the edge of the block to the saw blade should equal the desired length of the workpiece you're cutting. Make a test cut after the block is in place, and adjust the position of the block if needed.

2 Position the workpiece against the saw fence, with the end pressed firmly against the edge of the stop block. Hold the workpiece securely with your left hand and draw the blade over the board to make your cut. Wait until the blade has stopped spinning before you remove the workpiece and reset for your next cut.

WOODWORKING SKILLS
Pinning mortise-and-tenon joints with offset dowels

Pinning a mortise-and-tenon joint with offset dowels is a little-used joinery technique that you'll enjoy having in your bag of tricks. Instead of drilling straight through the assembled joint to drive in a standard through dowel, the dowel holes are drilled separately in the mortise and the tenon, and at a slight offset from one another. Because of the offset, when the joint is assembled and the dowel pin driven through, the pin will pull the parts of the joint together. This creates an exceptionally tight joint and can even eliminate the need for clamping.

Cut the mortises (See previous page) and the tenons (See *Tenoning jig*, page 50) as you would for any mortise-and-tenon joint. Prepare the dowel pins by cutting lengths of hardwood doweling that are the same length as the thickness of the board containing the mortise—it helps if you chamfer the lead end of the dowel. To make the joint, follow the instructions below. NOTE: *Make sure the dowel hole in the tenon is offset toward the tenon shoulder, not toward the end of the tenon.*

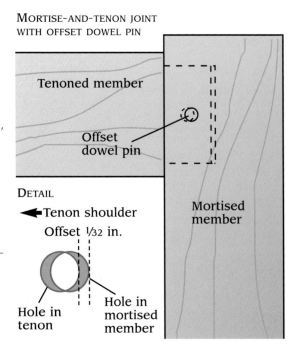

MORTISE-AND-TENON JOINT WITH OFFSET DOWEL PIN

Tenoned member

Offset dowel pin

Mortised member

DETAIL

◄─ Tenon shoulder

Offset ¹⁄₃₂ in.

Hole in tenon

Hole in mortised member

HOW TO PIN A MORTISE-AND-TENON JOINT WITH OFFSET DOWELS

1 Cut the mortise and the tenon and make sure the joint fits together cleanly. Mark a drilling point on the mortised workpiece, centered over the mortise. With a brad-point bit equal to the diameter of the dowel pin, drill a dowel hole into the workpiece. Set the depth stop so the dowel hole stops before exiting the other side of the workpiece.

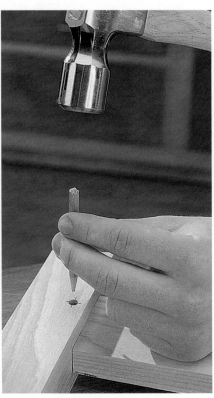

2 Insert the tenon into the mortise, then insert a sharpened dowel into the dowel hole and rap it lightly with a mallet or hammer to mark the location of the dowel hole on the tenon.

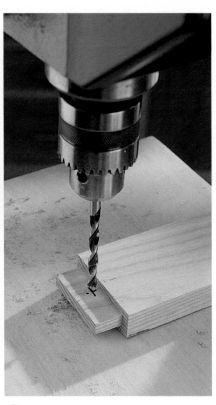

3 Remove the tenon and mark a drilling point that's aligned with the marked point on the tenon, but about ¹⁄₃₂ in. closer to the tenon shoulder. Drill all the way through the drilling point, then glue and reassemble the joint. Drive a dowel pin into the dowel hole, drawing the workpieces together. Trim off the end of the dowel so it's flush.

Resawing lumber on a band saw

Purchasing hardwood lumber that's less than ¾ in. thick is not economical—if you can even find it. But many woodworking projects require wood parts made of thinner stock. One option is to buy the thicker stock and plane or sand it down to thickness. But this is time-consuming and quite wasteful. A better option is to resaw the lumber into thinner strips on your band saw.

Most band saws come with a rip fence that attaches to the saw table. As long as you fit your saw with a suitable blade (a ¾-in.-wide, 6 tooth-per-in. hook-tooth blade is recommended) you can have some good success resawing lumber using only the rip fence as a guide (See *photo,* below). But for extra-thin stock, and to achieve results that require only a minimum of surface planing, we suggest using a resawing jig like the one shown here.

The greatest impediment to resawing lumber is wood grain. Even with a wide resawing blade installed, the blade naturally tries to follow the wood grain as you saw, following the path of least resistance. Forcing a board through the blade by pressing it against the rip fence generally doesn't solve this problem, as there is enough flex in the blade that it can still wander to some degree. The jig shown here contains a pivot point that's positioned next to the saw blade. The pivot point allows you to maintain a fairly consistent width of cut. At the same time, it gives you the opportunity to shift the workpiece from side to side as you feed it into the blade. By so doing, you can compensate for the wander in the blade by steering the workpiece back on line as the blade attempts to follow the grain.

Using this jig may sound like a fairly simple task, but as with any woodworking skill it requires some practice. Experiment with the jig before cutting your actual workpieces. Try making cuts of varying thickness in several different wood species until you feel comfortable with resawing, and you begin to get good results.

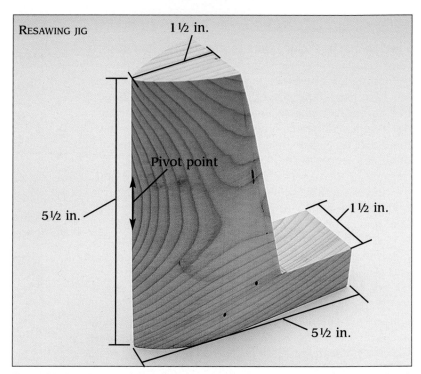

RESAWING JIG

1½ in.

Pivot point

5½ in.

1½ in.

5½ in.

This odd-looking jig is used as a guide when hand-feeding lumber for resawing on a band saw. The tail of the jig is clamped to the saw table. The tapered vertical surface is positioned perpendicular to the blade, creating a "fence" to steady the workpiece and help you maintain consistent thickness. The dimension can be adjusted according to the thickness of the stock you're resawing and the size of your band saw table. Make the jig on your band saw, and use a stationary sander to smooth out the cuts.

Resawing option: Using a band saw rip fence

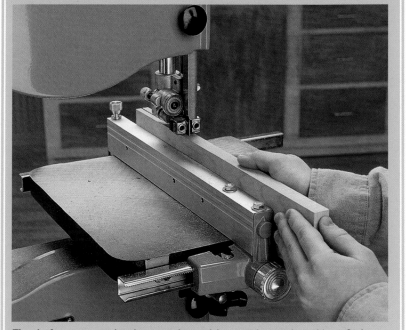

The rip fence on your band saw can be used for resawing stock as thin as ⅜ in. Run a test piece through first to make sure the fence is square to the blade, and make sure the blade guide is set slightly above the height of the workpiece. Plan on planing off at least ⅛ in. of material to smooth and square the resawn board.

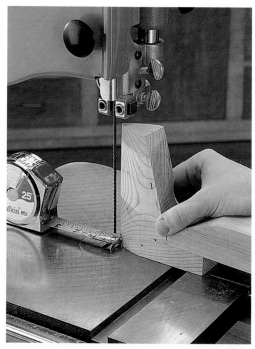

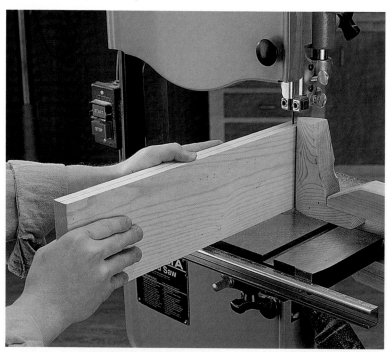

1 Make the resawing jig (See photo, previous page), then clamp it to the band saw table so the tapered point of the jig is perpendicular to the blade. The distance from the jig to the blade should equal the desired thickness of the workpiece, plus about 1/16 to 1/8 in. to allow for planing.

2 Use a marking gauge or a combination square to draw a cutting line along the edge of the board to be resawn. Turn on the saw and feed the workpiece into the blade with your right hand. Use your left hand to steer the workpiece against the pivot point, following the cutting line.

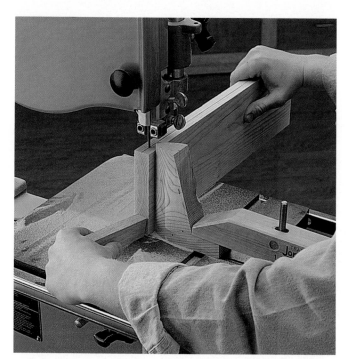

3 Be patient and don't worry about a little wandering—you'll need to surface plane the board at some point anyway, regardless of how careful you are. As you approach the end of the cut, use a push stick to push the board through. Be sure to keep the board steady by holding it on the outfeed side.

4 Set your thickness planer and plane both faces of the workpiece to remove the saw marks created by the band saw. Plane your stock in shallow, successive passes. Measure the thickness and continue planing until the workpiece is just right. Plane all same-thickness workpieces before changing the planer setup.

Resawing

HOW TO CUT CHAMFERS ON A DISC SANDER

Chamfering (vertical side tab)

1 Use any type of marking device (a marking gauge is shown here) to lay out guidelines for the bottoms of the chamfers. Mark each side of each workpiece.

WOODWORKING SKILLS
Chamfering with a disc sander

Chamfers are slanted cuts made at the edge of a workpiece to remove sharp edges. Cutting chamfers is an alternative to rounding over or breaking an edge with a sander or router. The choice of which method to use is mostly a matter of appearance. Chamfering is a good way to go if the project you're building has basically straight lines and square joints.

There are several methods for cutting chamfers. The most common is to use a router with a piloted chamfering bit. This is a good tool choice if you're chamfering long edges. You can also chamfer the edges of the individual workpieces before assembly, using a table saw with the blade set at a 45° angle (most chamfers are 45°). A more labor-intensive but time-honored method is to chamfer by hand with a block plane.

While these all are good techniques, we chose to use a stationary disc/belt sander to cut the chamfers shown here. Because they're cut in the tops of the workpiece, applying a router bit would be difficult and planing across end grain is always a chore. If you don't own a stationary disc sander, try mounting a hand-held sander to your workbench so the sanding area is perpendicular to the worksurface.

2 Check to make sure the table on your stationary disc sander is perpendicular to the sanding disc, then set the miter gauge on the table to a 45° angle (for 45° chamfers). Secure the miter gauge, then rest the workpiece on the table, flush against the miter gauge. Slowly engage the sanding disc with the workpiece. Sand until you've removed wood up to the cutting line.

3 Flip the workpiece over and repeat the procedure until the lines of the cuts are even on both faces. Continue flipping and repeating until all four sides are chamfered and the bottoms of the chamfers are even.

HOW TO UPHOLSTER A CHAIR SEAT

1 When the chair is assembled, measure the seat opening and cut a ½-in.-thick plywood seat base (the size depends on the project plan—if the seat board will fit inside a frame, make it slightly smaller than the opening to allow for the thickness of the upholstery material). Cut a piece of seat padding (1-in.-thick open-cell foam is being used above) the same size as the seat board. Cut a scrap from an old cotton sheet about 6 in. larger than the seat board on all sides. Lay the sheet on a flat, clean surface, with the foam and plywood on top. Wrap the sheet section around the seat board and cushion, as if you're wrapping a gift. There should be enough tension in the fabric to keep everything in place, but not so much that the fabric is strained. Staple the edges of the sheet to the underside of the seat board.

WOODWORKING SKILLS
Upholstering a chair seat

Working with upholstery is not very high on most handymen's list of favorite jobs. But if you're serious about making your own furniture, it's a very valuable skill to have. And the good news is with most furniture types you can do your own upholstering without ever needing to turn on a sewing machine or pull out needle and thread.

Seat boards for chairs, benches and even small sofas are easy to upholster—if you can gift-wrap a birthday present, you can upholster a chair seat. You simply lay the appropriate layers of material and padding over the board and secure them from below with staples or upholstery tacks. It's important to keep an eye on the visible side of the seat as you work, though, especially if you're working with patterned upholstery material.

2 Then cut a piece of upholstery that's also about 6 in. larger than the seat on all sides. If using printed upholstery, pay attention to the pattern before cutting. Staple one edge of the material to the seat board, then draw the opposite edge tight and staple it securely.

3 Make sure the pattern is centered and well positioned. Fold over the adjoining edges, pulling the fabric snugly and stapling as you go. Work from the centers toward the corners. Trim off excess fabric at the corners with a scissors, then fold the corners as neatly as you can before stapling them down. Trim off any excess fabric, then attach the seat to the chair frame.

Walnut Coffee Table

Rich oiled walnut and dramatic veneer inlays combine to create an exceptionally striking coffee table. Nicely proportioned with a generous shelf below, this is a truly unique project that will undoubtedly become a cherished family heirloom. Building it is a very special woodworking experience that contains numerous techniques and tricks you'll use over and over again.

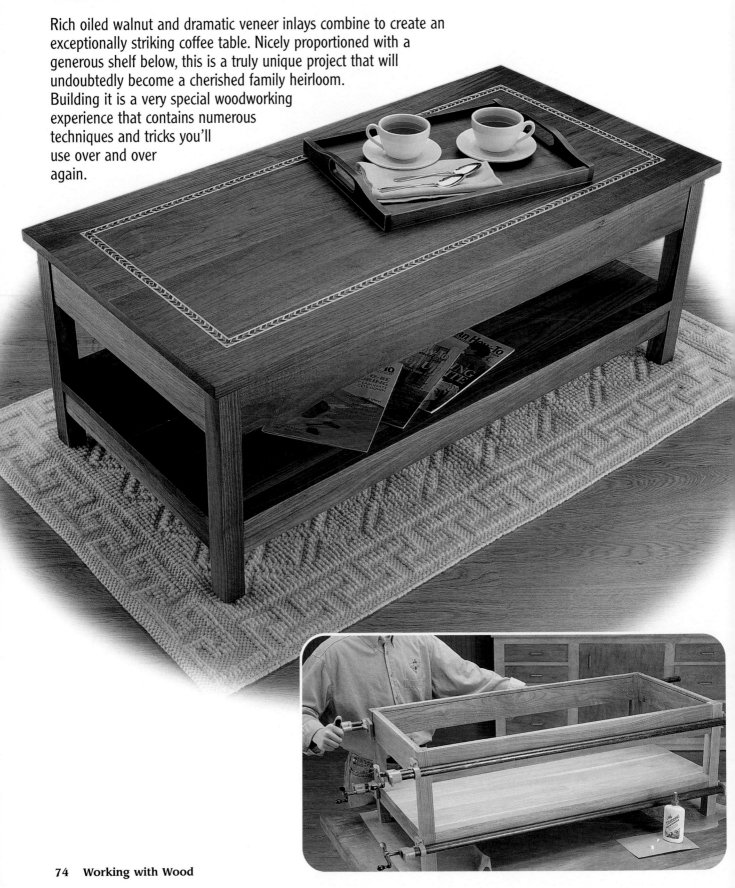

Woodworking Skills You'll Learn:

- Designing a coffee table

- Clamping a table frame

- Using biscuits or dowels as alignment aids

- Rounding tenons

• Inlaying decorative veneer strips

• Scraping and sanding a glued-up wood panel

• Attaching tabletops with table clips

• Edge-gluing wood panels

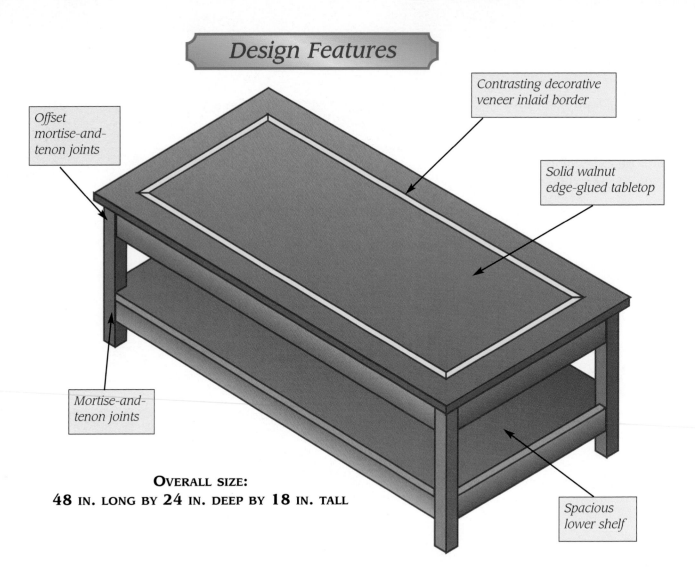

Offset mortise-and-tenon joints

Contrasting decorative veneer inlaid border

Solid walnut edge-glued tabletop

Mortise-and-tenon joints

Spacious lower shelf

OVERALL SIZE:
48 IN. LONG BY 24 IN. DEEP BY 18 IN. TALL

PROJECT NO. 4:

Walnut Coffee Table

The strength of this walnut coffee table is in its simplicity and its lustrous appearance. The large, 2-ft. × 4-ft. tabletop is made of slabs of solid walnut resting on a simple frame. A clear finish allows the natural color and beauty of the walnut to shine through. The dark walnut contrasts with an inlaid border of decorative veneer strips for a truly dynamic affect.

General planning

The coffee table is a relatively new entry in the gallery of American furniture. You won't find many coffee tables listed among the designs of the better known furniture styles. The few guidelines that do exist for designing a coffee table are quite general, relating mostly to height and surface area ranges. In effect, when you sit down to design a coffee table, almost anything goes.

Parts of a coffee table. Like other tables, the most

prominent feature of a coffee table is the *tabletop*. Most coffee tables made in the woodshop are fitted with tops made of either glued-up panels or veneered plywood. An *apron* can be found on many tables, forming a frame that joins the underside of the tabletop. The apron boards connect the tops of the *legs*. *Stretchers,* sometimes called *spreaders,* connect the legs closer to the bottoms, helping to keep the framework square. A lower shelf or even an enclosed cabinet can be added.

Dimensions. Coffee tables can be built in a wide range of sizes, depending on the length and seat height of the sofa, the available space in the room, and the general appearance you're looking to create. Generally, casual coffee tables are broader and shorter than more formal table designs—mostly because the same holds true for sofas. Make sure the table will fit the space, allowing at least 8 inches of leg room between the table and the sofa, and plenty of clear walking space on the opposite side. Also bear in mid that higher tables are easier to use for setting down your beverage or serving food. The most common heights range from 12 to 20 inches, and the depth from front to back is usually about 20 inches, give or take a few. The table shown here is 18 inches high, 24 inches deep and a full 48 inches long.

Material. We built this coffee table from solid black walnut—an exceptionally rich wood that is one of a woodworker's most prized commodities. Grown and harvested in the United States and Canada, walnut has a dark brown color with streaks of light and dark browns and blacks throughout. Walnut furniture enriches a room in a way matched only by more expensive imported exotic woods such as teak and mahogany and even rosewood. Whether you use solid walnut or walnut-veneered plywood, walnut can be used for furniture and cabinets in any room in the house. For a subtle decorative touch, we inlaid 1-in.-wide patterned veneer strips in a rectangular border pattern. These strips are available in numerous colors, patterns and widths from woodworking stores and catalogs.

Cherry and mahogany are used frequently for building formal coffee tables. Oak and maple create a versatile look that can work in either a formal or a casual setting. Pine is a very popular wood for coffee tables as well, particularly in the informal "Country" styles.

Aesthetics. Shape, proportion and decoration are the primary variables that affect the look of a coffee table. They range from low, square boxes, sometimes with cabinet doors, to high, narrow tables with contoured or carved legs and decorative scrollwork or fretwork on the aprons. Select a style that blends with the other furnishings in your home, and that's manageable with your woodworking tools and skills. The design shown here is based on square joints and simple lines, giving it a slightly contemporary appearance. But the dark tones of the oiled walnut allow the table to work in a more traditional setting as well.

Construction details

The walnut tabletop and shelf are the critical pieces when building this table. Although the table frame, particularly the legs and aprons, are visible, the top dominates and deserves the most attention.

About walnut

Once one of the more common and popular hardwoods, walnut has suffered from overharvesting more than many other species, and has become somewhat scarce (and fairly expensive). Even so, walnut remains an excellent woodworking investment. For richness of color and wood grain, it's virtually unmatched among American hardwoods.

Grain: The grain is relatively straight with a medium density. The grain lines are very dark brown to black.

Color: Dark brown with variations of light and dark browns and black streaks. Sapwood tends to be lighter in tone than heartwood, which can cause significant color change in a single plain-sawn board.

Workability: The straight grain makes walnut moderately easy to work with, although the grain density can cause some wear on cutting edges.

Finishing: The relatively smooth grain texture allows walnut to absorb stains evenly, but stains tend to obscure rather than enhance the grain. Therefore, walnut is generally finished with a clear finish, such as Danish Oil or lacquer, to accent the grain.

Unfinished

With clear oil applied

Black walnut

EDGE-GLUED PANEL WITH REINFORCING BISCUITS

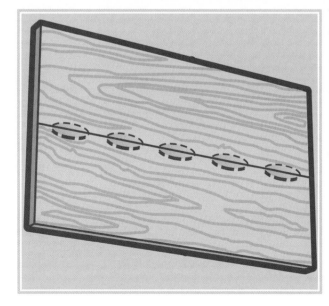

The tabletop and shelf are made by edge-gluing walnut boards into wide panels, then cutting the panels to size. We used biscuits at the joints where the boards are joined. The main purpose of the biscuits is to keep the boards aligned during glue-up, but they do provide some extra strength by increasing glue coverage.

About Inlays

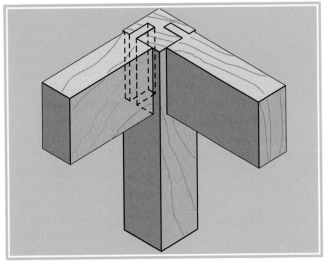

Most woodworking stores and catalogs sell a variety of decorative veneer inlay strips. The inlay strips are made of 1/32-in.-thick veneers applied to a paper backing. Available in widths from less than 1/8 in. to more than 1 in. wide, commercial inlays consist of regional and exotic contrasting woods such as maple, walnut, ebony and satinwood. Most of the varieties you'll find have strong geometric patterns. You can also purchase veneer inlay strips dyed in solid colors. Or, you can use raw strips of naturally contrasting wood (for example, maple inlay strips set into a walnut surface). Inlays are applied with wood glue after a surface is completely prepared, but before the finish has been applied.

OFFSET MORTISE-AND-TENON JOINT

The tenons on an offset mortise-and-tenon joint are cut closer to the outer face of the board so the bottoms of the two mortises are as far apart as possible.

The tabletop is edge-glued together from several narrow boards. To keep the number of seams to a minimum, use the widest boards you can find. Look for interesting grain patterns and color variations, and visualize how you'll match the different grain patterns. The best way to get a uniform appearance throughout the glued-up panel is to use either a single long board cut into shorter sections, or to use boards milled in successive cuts from the same log (in many cases, these boards will still be next to one another in the lumber stack). The shelf is also edge-glued, but reserve your better lumber for the tabletop. To save a few dollars, you could build the shelf from walnut-veneer plywood with edges wrapped in veneer edge tape.

The most important joints n any table are the ones between the legs and the aprons. Here, we used offset mortise-and-tenon joints with mortises that are open on top to connect the apron boards to the tops of the legs (See *Illustration*, left). The shelf aprons are joined to the legs with standard mortise and tenon joints.

There are several good ways to attach a tabletop to a table frame. The most important consideration is wood movement, especially if the tabletop is made from a glued-up panel. One simple attachment method is to install corner blocks with slot-shaped screw holes, then drive screws up through the blocks and into the tops (See Shaker-style Valet Table, page 45). For our coffee table, we chose to use table clips instead. These small pieces of hardware are screwed to the underside of the tabletop along the perimeter. They contain lips that project out and away from the tabletop. These lips are fitted into narrow grooves on the upper inside faces of the apron boards, where they are free to move in the slots as the tabletop expands and contracts.

To inlay the veneer strips in the tabletop, we used a router with a straight bit to cut very shallow grooves in the border area. Then we smoothed out the bottoms of the grooves with a narrow grooving plane. Cutting these grooves is perhaps the trickiest task you'll face building this project. The veneer strips are only 1/32 in. thick, so it's very easy to remove too much material. In that case, you'll have to apply wood filler into the groove, which can become a real mess. Once the grooves are cut, the trick becomes matching the veneer strips at the corners. Most decorative strips you'll find for sale have very geometric patterns that are designed to make symmetrical 45° corners—if they're positioned correctly. The best way to ensure that the corners look good is to make the corners first, then butt-join the ends of the strips somewhere in the middle of each run.

For a durable wood finish (you'll want plenty of protection from heat and moisture on a coffee table top), we used our own blend of turpentine, boiled linseed oil and varnish.

Coffee table style variations

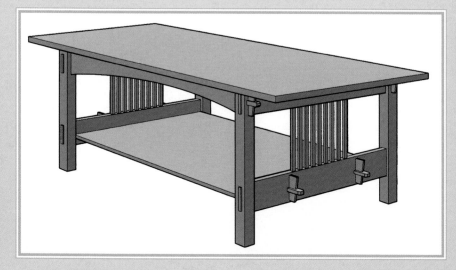

This Arts-and-Crafts style table is distinguished by slatted frets on the ends and tenoned spreaders that are secured with exposed tenon pins. In dimensions and proportion, it's similar to the table featured in this chapter, although the styling is a considerable departure. Typically, a table of this style is built in quarter-sawn white oak, and will have a relatively dark finish.

A more traditional furnishing, this old-style tea table is taller and generally more frail in appearance than more contemporary coffee tables. But with the delicately shaped legs and the decorative contours on the apron, it has a formal look that's accentuated if built from cherry or mahogany.

A Country style coffee table is right at home in any casual setting. Made of pine or oak, it's expansive tabletop is nearly square in proportion. What minimal style it possesses is drawn mostly from the heavy, round legs that are spindle-turned on a lathe.

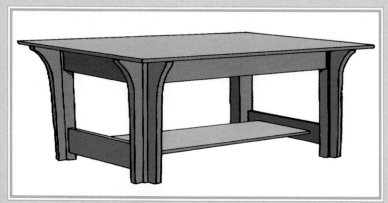

The heavy proportions of this oak coffee table make it a focal point of any room. Although the legs are actually made from 1-in-thick stock, the broad "L" shape of each leg assembly gives the illusion of much heavier wood stock.

More of an end table than a coffee table, this Arts-and-Crafts table could serve as a coffee table if placed in front of one of the high, rigid sofas common to the style. Or, it would fit nicely between a sofa and an arm chair.

COFFEE TABLE

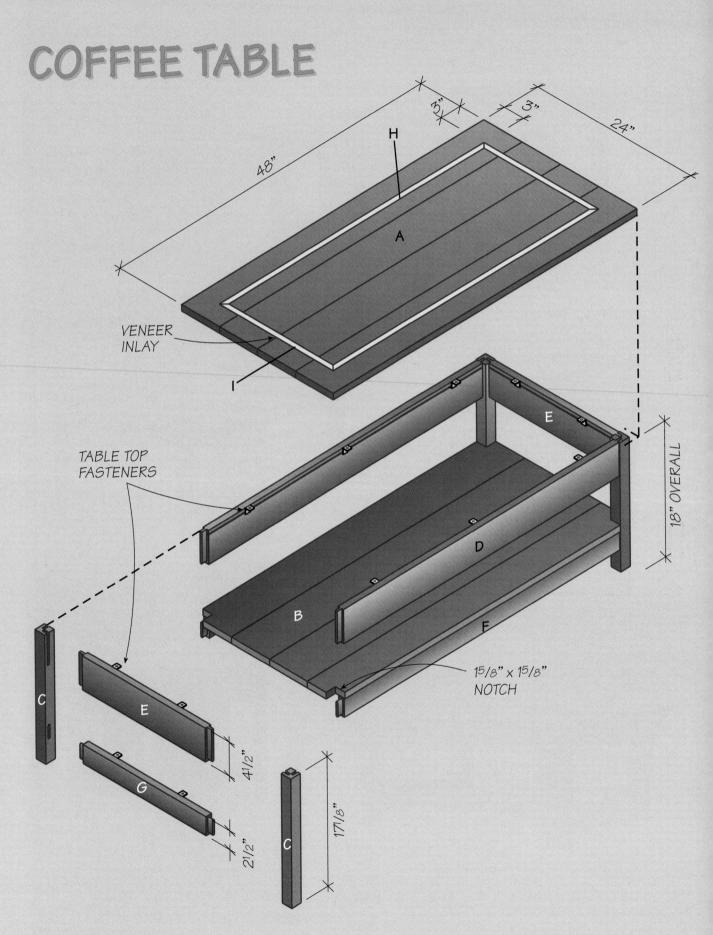

48"

3"

3"

24"

H

A

VENEER
INLAY

I

TABLE TOP
FASTENERS

E

D

18" OVERALL

B

F

15/8" x 15/8"
NOTCH

C

E

G

C

41/2"

21/2"

171/8"

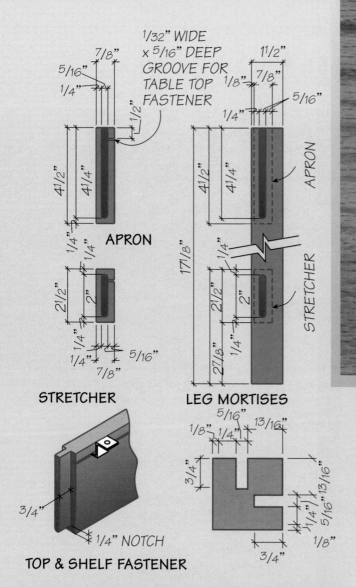

1/32" WIDE x 5/16" DEEP GROOVE FOR TABLE TOP FASTENER

7/8"
5/16"
1/4"
1/2"
4 1/2"
4 1/4"

APRON

1 1/2"
1/8"
7/8"
1/4"
5/16"
4 1/2"
4 1/4"

APRON

17 1/8"
1/4"
2 1/2"
2"
2 7/8"
1/4"

STRETCHER

2 1/2"
2"
1/4"
1/4"
5/16"
7/8"

STRETCHER

LEG MORTISES

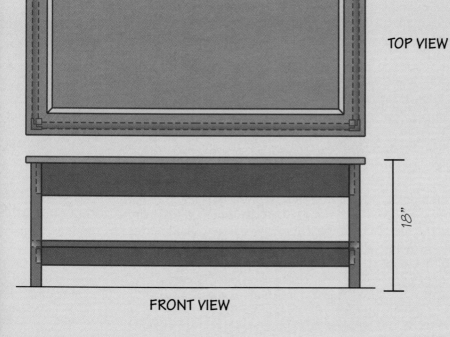

TOP & SHELF FASTENER

3/4"
1/4" NOTCH

5/16"
13/16"
1/8"
1/4"
3/4"
5/16"
13/16"
1/4"
1/8"
3/4"

TOP VIEW

FRONT VIEW

SIDE VIEW

18"

24"

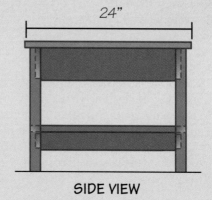

Walnut Coffee Table Cutting List

Part		No.	Size	Material
A.	Top	1	7/8 × 24 × 48"	Walnut
B.	Shelf	1	7/8 × 22 1/2 × 46 1/2"	"
C.	Legs	4	1 1/2 × 1 1/2 × 17 1/8"	"
D.	Long Aprons	2	7/8 × 4 1/2 × 45"	"
E.	Short Aprons	2	7/8 × 4 1/2 × 21"	"
F.	Long Stretchers	2	7/8 × 2 1/2 × 45"	"
G.	Short Stretchers	2	7/8 × 2 1/2 × 21"	"
H.	Inlay, Top	2	3/4 wide × 42"*	
I.	Inlay, Top	2	3/4 wide × 18"*	

*Cut to fit after routing inlay grooves.

Project Assembly Steps: Walnut Coffee Table

Glue-up the tabletop & shelves

1 Select the boards for gluing-up the tabletop and shelf (See *Edge-gluing*, page 86). Surface plane the boards so they're equal in thickness and smooth on both faces.

2 Joint both edges of each board on your jointer or with a jointing plane. Arrange the boards for gluing, alternating the direction of the growth rings to prevent cupping.

3 Prepare the mating edges of the boards for reinforcement. We cut slots for biscuit joints spaced at about 8 in. intervals (See page 77). You could use dowels instead. The primary goal is to keep the boards aligned during glue-up.

4 Insert the biscuits or dowels, then apply glue to the mating edges of the glue-ups. Clamp the glued-up panels together with pipe clamps or bar clamps, alternating the clamps above and below the assemblies. To keep the panels from cupping as the glue dries, we sandwiched them between hardwood cauls at regular intervals along the panel **(See FIGURE A)**. Let the panels dry overnight.

5 Unclamp and smooth out the panels (See page 88). Keep them in a flat position until you're ready to finish making the parts.

Make the legs

1 Make the legs, either by thickness planing ⁸⁄₄ stock or by face-gluing two pieces of surfaced stock (See *Face-gluing*, page 46). When the leg blanks dry, run one edge of each blank through your jointer, then rip-cut the the blank to 1½ in. square on your table saw. Crosscut the legs to length (17⅛ in.).

FIGURE A: Edge-glue panels for the tabletop and the shelf. Use biscuits or dowels to align the butt joints in the glue-up. Sandwiching the panels between hardwood cauls helps prevent cupping and keeps the boards aligned.

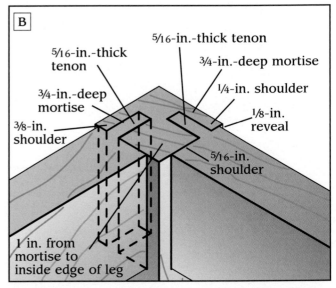

FIGURE B: The offset mortise-and-tenon joints where the legs join the aprons can be tricky to cut. Both the tenons and the mortises are 4¼ in. long—you'll need to remove the bottom ¼ in. of the tenon.

2 Lay out the mortises for the aprons and the stretchers in each leg (See *diagram*, page 81, and **FIGURE B**). Note that the mortises are offset: they're closer to the outside edges of the legs than the inside edges.

3 Cut the mortises. Because all the mortises are ⁵⁄₁₆ in. thick, we cut them with a plunge router

FIGURE C: Glue together the two end assemblies for the table frame, and clamp with padded pipe clamps. Measure the diagonals to make sure they're square.

FIGURE D: Dry-assemble the long stretchers and aprons between the two end assemblies so you can check to make sure the parts all fit and, at the same time, take accurate measurements for cutting the shelf to final size.

and 5/16 in. straight bit (See *How to cut mortises with a plunge router,* page 49). Don't square off the ends of the mortises. It's easier and cleaner to round the ends of the tenons to fit, as shown above.

Make the aprons & stretchers

1 Cut the aprons and the stretchers to size. Cut a few scrap pieces that are the same thickness and width as the aprons and the tenons to use as test pieces. Select and mark whichever face of each board you want to be visible.

2 Make a tenoning jig and set up your table saw to cut the tenons (See *Mortise-and-tenon joints,* pages 48 to 49). The tenons should be the same thickness (5/16 in.) and depth (3/4 in.) on all the workpieces (See *diagram,* page 81 and **FIGURE B**). Like the mortises, the tenons also are offset. The shoulder on the good side of each workpiece is 1/4 in. wide and the shoulder on the inside face is 5/16 in. wide. These dimensions presume the workpieces are 7/8 in. thick and the mortises are 5/16 in. thick. Cut test pieces until they match the mortises. If the fit is good, the tenon will be snug but you won't need to force it into the mortise.

3 Cut the tenons in the aprons and stretchers. After all the tenons are cut, trim the corners of the tenons with a chisel, rounding them so they'll fit into the mortises (See *TIP,* above).

4 Cut 1/8-in.-wide grooves for the clips that will be used to attach the tabletop and shelf. The clips we used require 5/16-in.-deep grooves cut 1/2 in. down from the top edges.

Assemble the table frame

1 Glue and clamp the mortise-and-tenon joints to form the two ends of the table frame (**See FIGURE C**). Test to make sure the joints are square by measuring the diagonals.

2 Dry-assemble the long aprons and stretchers between the end assemblies (**See FIGURE D**). Check to make sure all the joints fit together cleanly, and measure the diagonals to check for square (once you've glued the parts together, it's tough to go back in and make adjustments).

3 Because the shelf is very broad and the space between the aprons and stretchers is fairly narrow, you'll have to assemble the coffee table with the shelf in rough position. But first, you'll need to cut the shelf to size and make notches in the corners that fit around the legs. To accomplish both tasks accurately, lay the dry assembly upside-down on the shelf. Center the assembly on the shelf, then trace around the inside faces of the legs to mark outlines for the notches **(See FIGURE E)**.

4 Remove the dry-assembly, then draw cutting lines ⅛ in. larger and cut out the notches with a jig saw. Check the fit by dry-assembling the table frame with the shelf in place. Enlarging the notches allows the shelf to expand

5 Glue the frame together with the shelf in rough position **(See FIGURE F)**. Use at least two pipe clamps per side, and check the diagonals for aquare. After removing the clamps, you may attach the shelf with the table clips. Or, you can wait to do it at the same time as you attach the tabletop.

FIGURE E: Set the table frame onto the underside of the shelf and trace around the inside faces of the legs to position the shelf notches. Then cut the notches ⅛ in. larger to allow for shelf wood movement.

Make the tabletop

1 Trim the tabletop to the finished dimensions, then sand and finish-sand all surfaces using progressively finer sandpaper (up to 180 grit).

2 Prepare to install the decorative veneer inlays (See *Inlaying veneer,* page 89). Lay out a border frame for the inlays. We positioned them so the outer edges are 3 in. from the edges of the tabletop all around.

3 Using a router with a 1 in.straight bit (the diameter of the bit should match the thickness of the inlay strips), make a ¹⁄₃₂-in.-deep test cut in a piece of scrap and lay a veneer strip into the groove. The inlay should be flush with the surrounding surface. Adjust the cutting depth until it's properly set, then clamp a straightedge guide to the tabletop and position a stop at each end of the channel to avoid cutting too far. Carefully rout grooves inside the border outline **(See FIGURE G)**.

4 Square the corners of the channel with a wood chisel, then lightly smooth the bottom of the channel with a grooving plane (See page 89).

5 Lay the inlay strips in the channel, starting at a corner. Cut the strips with a utility knife, miter-

FIGURE F: With the shelf in position, glue and clamp the table frame together. Measure the diagonals and adjust as needed until the frame is precisely square.

FIGURE G: Carefully rout a channel for the decorative veneer inlays. Use a straightedge guide to keep the router on course, and position stop blocks at each end of each cut to keep yourself from routing too far.

FIGURE H: After gluing the inlay strips into the channels, cover the strips with wax paper, then clamp pieces of plywood over them to ensure that they are well-bonded and that they lay flat.

FIGURE I: Attach the tabletop to the frame with table clips. Insert the lips of the clips into the grooves in the apron, then fasten the clips to the tabletop with wood screws.

FIGURE J: Apply the wood finish after the table is completely assembled. We used a home-made finish made of boiled linseed oil, turpentine and varnish (See TIP, page 11).

cutting the corners. Paying attention to the decorative pattern, cut the inlay strips to fit (See *Inlaying veneer,* page 89).

6 Tape the strips in place, then remove, glue and replace them one at a time. Spread the glue evenly in the channel, and wipe away squeeze-out immediately. After the inlays are all in position, clamp plywood strips directly on the inlays (**See FIGURE H**). Insert wax paper between the plywood strips and inlays.

Finishing touches
Lay the tabletop upside-down on a flat surface and attach it to the frame with table clips fitted into the grooves in the apron (**See FIGURE I**). Sand the tabletop and all wood surfaces with a random-orbit sander and 180-grit paper to prepare it for finishing. You can go as high as 220-grit if you like. Remove the sawdust with a tack cloth, then finish the table (**See FIGURE J**). We used a home-made oil-based finish designed to accent the tone and grain of the walnut .

Edge-gluing panels

Gluing-up wide panels from narrow boards is a valuable, if not essential, woodworking skill. These days, it's often difficult to find stock wider than 6 inches, particularly in the more exotic hardwoods. But since most projects call for parts that are wider than 6 inches, your best, most economical recourse is to glue two or more narrower strips into a wide panel.

Selecting the best stock for edge-gluing is critical to the final appearance of the panel. When possible, try to cut strips from the same board or two boards that were taken in successive cuts from the log. Obviously, any stock with defects should be avoided. Look for consistent color and grain pattern, keeping in mind that you'll want to arrange the boards with their growth rings in alternating directions (this helps prevent cupping).

There are several techniques for edge-gluing panels, each with its own advantages. The easiest way to edge-glue boards is to use alignment aids, such as biscuits, dowels or splines. Alignment aids help to keep the boards flush while you glue-up. There is some debate over whether they contribute to the strength of the joint. There doesn't appear to be any evidence that they do make a difference.

Edge-gluing with biscuits. Using biscuits (sometimes called "plates") is a nearly foolproof alignment method. The biscuits, made of compressed wood products, are actually smaller than the slots you cut for them. Once the biscuits come in contact with moisture (i.e., glue), they expand to form a very tight joint. The time between inserting the biscuits and applying the clamps is ample to allow you to maneuver the boards side-to-side to make sure your layout lines align. Once the joint is set, the biscuits assure that the boards stay aligned top-to-bottom.

Edge-gluing with dowels. Dowels are used frequently for edge-gluing panels, partly because not everyone owns a biscuit joiner. The basic procedure is the same as with a biscuit joiner. To align the dow-

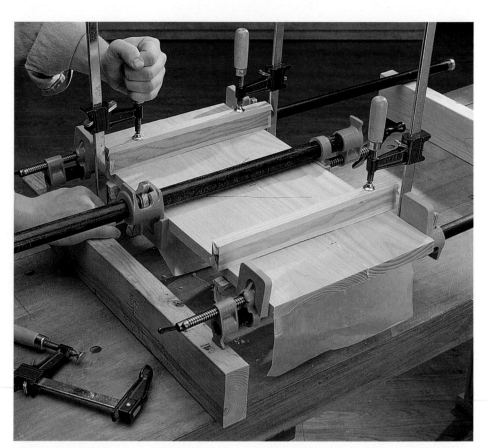

When gluing-up, use bar or pipe clamps every 10 or 12 inches, alternating the clamps so one bar is beneath the assembly, the next one above it, and so on. Use only enough pressure so a small amount of glue squeezes out. especially if you're not using biscuits or dowels to align the boards, use large C-clamps or smaller bar clamps to clamp wood cauls to the assembly and flush the joints. Use cauls in pairs—one above and one below the panel. If the cauls fail to bring the surfaces flush, loosen the horizontal clamps until the caul clamps bring the surfaces flush, then retighten the horizontal clamps.

els, you can simply use metal dowel points inserted in the first set of holes on one edge. Press the boards together and you've got precise drilling points for the mating dowel holes. But a more reliable way to make dowel joints is to use a doweling jig (See the photos on the following page and *Dowel joints,* page 30).

Edge-gluing without alignment aids. Edge-gluing boards without any alignment aids requires only a little more advance preparation than using biscuits, dowels or splines. Namely, prepare some ¾-in.-thick × 1½-in.-wide wood cauls that are at least a few inches longer than the width of the panel (See *photo* above). Make enough cauls so you can use one pair every 10 inches along the panel. Line the cauls with masking tape to keep them from sticking to the workpiece.

Smoothing the panel

Regardless of the technique and the amount of care you use, you'll need to smooth the panel and flush the joints after the glue dries. Use a cabinet scraper or hand plane, or a power sander for this. Avoid running glued-up panels through your power planer.

HOW TO PREPARE BOARDS FOR EDGE-GLUING

Alternate direction of growth rings

1 Once you've chosen your stock, joint all the edges so they're perfectly smooth and flat. A power jointer is the easiest tool for the job, although you can do the job by hand with a jointing plane. When using a power jointer, push the board down and forward on the infeed table with one hand, and use the other hand to press the board against the fence. Don't press down on the part of the board that has passed the cutterhead.

2 Arrange the jointed boards together to get the most pleasing match of the different grain patterns. This can take some trial and error. Be sure to alternate the direction of the growth rings at the ends of the boards. This helps keep the panel from cupping. Once you've got all the boards arranged to your satisfaction, draw a "V" across all joints in the panel. Use the legs of the "V" to maintain your alignment as you glue-up the panel.

HOW TO ALIGN BOARDS WITH BISCUITS

1 Once the boards are laid out and marked, place them in position and mark the biscuit locations. Use a square to mark all mating edges to ensure that the slots align. Biscuits should be spaced about 8 to 10 inches apart, with a biscuit about 2 inches in from each end. After marking biscuit locations, cut the slots by aligning your marks with the permanent mark on the biscuit joiner.

2 Apply glue to one edge of each board to be joined, then squeeze glue into the slots. Commercial glue applicators that reach into the slots are available, or you can simply squeeze the glue in with a regular glue bottle and spread the glue with a homemade spreader (a piece of ⅛-inch-thick wood or a clean popsicle stick work well). Add the biscuits to the slots on one board. If edge-gluing more than one board at a time, apply the glue and insert the biscuits in every board. Now you're ready to clamp the assembly.

HOW TO ALIGN BOARDS WITH DOWELS

1 Joint all edges, then drill dowel holes (⅜ in. dia. holes are most common and can be used with stock ¾-in. thick and thicker) in one edge, spaced at 8 to 10 inch intervals. Use a doweling jig or metal dowel points to drill matching dowel holes in the mating edge.

2 Apply glue to the ends of fluted hardwood dowels (See Dowel joints, page 30) and drive them into the dowel holes in one edge, using a wood mallet. Apply glue to the edges of the boards and to the free ends of the dowel. Press the boards together and clamp.

OPTIONS FOR SMOOTHING THE SURFACE OF A GLUED-UP PANEL

Use a cabinet scraper. If the surface is fairly flat, you can remove the dried glue and even-out minor joint ridges with a sharp cabinet scraper. Lay a metal straightedge across the surface to determine if there are high and low spots. If so, use a jack plane on smaller surfaces or a smoothing plane on larger surfaces to smooth the surface after removing the dried glue. Plane at a 45° angle to the joints until you've knocked off all the high points. Finish smoothing the surface with the cabinet scraper and, if desired, a random-orbit sander.

Use a belt sander. A belt sander can make quick work of evening-out a panel with boards that aren't quite flush. Avoid using belts coarser than 100 grit, and sand in a diagonal direction to the grain pattern. A good trick for belt sanding a panel is to mark any high spots with squiggly pencil lines, then sand until the lines are gone and re-check with a straightedge. After belt sanding, you'll need to use an orbital sander with finer paper to remove the sanding marks.

WOODWORKING SKILLS

Inlaying veneer strips

Inlaid veneer strips can provide a touch of elegance, even excitement, to an otherwise ordinary woodworking project. Sold in woodworking stores and catalogs, the strips come in a wide variety of sizes, colors and patterns (See page 78). Inlaying them into your project requires some patience and care, as there is very little margin for error when working on such a small scale. Working with the patterns on veneer strips is a little like hanging patterned wallpaper—the success of the task depends largely on how well you plan the layout and how accurately you cut the corners and seams.

HOW TO INLAY VENEER STRIPS

1 Outline a border frame for the inlays. Rout a channel for each strip, following the outline. The cutting depth should equal the thickness of the strips (usually 1/32 in.) and the bit diameter should equal the width of the strips (from 1/4 to 1 in.) Use a straightedge guide and clamp stop blocks at the ends of the channels.

2 After routing, use a small grooving plane to clean up the bottom of the channel. For narrower strips, you may prefer to cut the entire channel with the grooving plane—be sure to use a straightedge. Most catalog companies that sell veneer strips also carry grooving planes in a range of sizes.

3 Square the corners of the channel with a chisel, then lay the inlay strips, starting at a corner. Carefully make a 45° miter cut at the corner, paying attention to the pattern. Cut all your pieces, tape them in place, then remove them one at a time for gluing.

4 Press the strips into the channels to seat them in the glue (you can use a wallpaper seam roller here). Cover the strips with wax paper, then clamp strips of plywood over the inlays to hold them in place while the glue sets. Carefully scrape off dried glue when done.

Armoire Entertainment Center

The traditional look of this oak armoire cabinet belies the fact that inside you'll find roomy and plentiful accomodations for the most state-of-the-art electronic components. A simple cabinet fashioned from oak plywood and biscuit joints, this entertainment center features just enough detailing to give it a sense of style all its own.

- **Building a cornice out of crown molding**

- **Boring adjustable shelf pin holes with a shop-made jig**

- **Cutting double-dado joints**

- **Installing European-style concealed door hinges**

• **Applying iron-on veneer edge tape**

• **Building shelves with wood stiffeners**

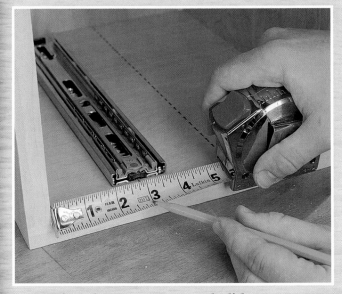

• **Hanging drawers on metal slides**

• **Making biscuit joints**

Design Features

OVERALL DIMENSIONS:
74 IN. HIGH BY
36 IN. WIDE BY
24 IN. DEEP

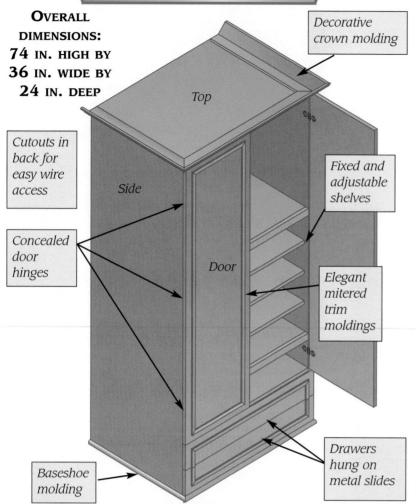

Decorative crown molding

Top

Cutouts in back for easy wire access

Side

Fixed and adjustable shelves

Concealed door hinges

Door

Elegant mitered trim moldings

Baseshoe molding

Drawers hung on metal slides

PROJECT NO. 5

Armoire Entertainment Center

This innovative armoire-style entertainment center offers the best of both worlds: traditional styling coupled with modern conveniences. An oak plywood carcase houses ample space and shelving for any electronic technology enthusiast. Just pull open the twin cabinet doors for immediate access to your television and stereo systems.

General planning

Designing an entertainment center starts with taking inventory of your equipment—what you own currently, as well as whatever else you hope to add in the future. This will give you a rough idea of the size requirements. But because the entertainment center is also a highly visible piece of furniture, it's important to assess the look and style of the other furnishings it will be near. And don't forget to keep the size of the room in mind: efficient entertainment centers can quickly become television shrines if you don't keep proportions in mind.

Armoire style variations

Old-fashioned wardrobe with frame-and-panel doors, milled cornice and decorative scrollwork at base. Design would require deepening to serve as an entertainment center.

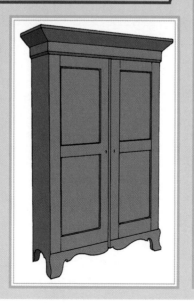

This two-part cupboard with breakfront would require some adaptation to serve as either an armoire or an entertainment center, but the decorative doors and the interesting base profiles offer a good starting point for any design.

Parts of an armoire. The armoire entertainment center is basically a free-standing cabinet with a *carcase, shelves, cabinet doors* and *drawers*. This design also features a decorative cornice on top of the cabinet, made from crown molding. The interior has several fixed shelves, adjustable shelves and a partition, all positioned to house the drawers and components. The partition between the TV shelf and the component shelf provides support from which to hang the adjustable shelves. The adjustable shelves to the right of the partition are wide enough for the electronic components. The shelves to the left can hold CDs, tapes, books, photos, etc.

Dimensions. We wanted our armoire to hold a 27-in. television, currently the most popular selling size in America, and the usual electronic components (See *Design specs,* below). We also wanted storage space for CDs and cassette and VCR tapes. Using 4 × 8 plywood sheets, we laid out a plywood cutting diagram that yielded the dimensions we needed (See page 96) to create just the right amount of shelf space for all the components.

Materials. We used oak-veneer plywood to build this project. The only non-plywood parts are the trim moldings.

Aesthetics. A plywood cabinet has the straight lines associated with contemporary design. To give the armoire a more traditional look, we've added oak crown molding at the top, shoe molding at the base and strips of solid oak cabinet molding to the doors and drawer faces. You can eliminate the moldings entirely for a clean, contemporary look.

Construction details

Butt joints reinforced with biscuits do most of the work in this plywood project. The fixed TV and component shelves bear a heavy load and will sag unless stiffened (See *Design specs,* page 17). The other fixed horizontal pieces bear no weight beyond their own. The adjustable shelves are only 13⅛ and 18 in. wide and require no extra support.

All of the moldings used to decorate the armoire—cornice, door and drawer face, and shoe (base) moldings—are mitered at 45° at the corner joints. Each 45° miter equals half of the 90° corner where the moldings meet, forming a perfect corner joint. Mitering allows all of the various molding profiles to meet without exposing any end grain. The armoire drawers are large and will carry heavy loads, so we used double-dado joints, with their increased gluing area and strong mechanical bond. The drawer face is a false front, installed after the drawers are built and hung with metal glides.

About oak plywood

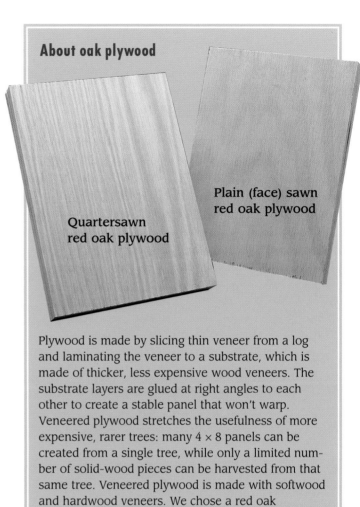

Quartersawn red oak plywood

Plain (face) sawn red oak plywood

Plywood is made by slicing thin veneer from a log and laminating the veneer to a substrate, which is made of thicker, less expensive wood veneers. The substrate layers are glued at right angles to each other to create a stable panel that won't warp. Veneered plywood stretches the usefulness of more expensive, rarer trees: many 4 × 8 panels can be created from a single tree, while only a limited number of solid-wood pieces can be harvested from that same tree. Veneered plywood is made with softwood and hardwood veneers. We chose a red oak veneered plywood, although you can use birch, ash, pine, walnut or any number of available veneered plywoods. The face veneer, on the good side of the plywood, is a better grade with fewer defects and better matching of veneer strips than the veneer on the flip side. Look for quartersawn plywood veneer, especially if using oak plywood.

Design specs

Typical electronic component dimensions:

Component	Height	Width	Depth
Television (27")	23"	26"	20"
Receiver	5-6"	17"	12"
CD player	4-5"	17"	10-15"
Tape player	5"	17"	10"
Turntable	16" (opened)	17"	14"
VCR	3-5"	15-17"	11"

ARMOIRE ENTERTAINMENT CENTER

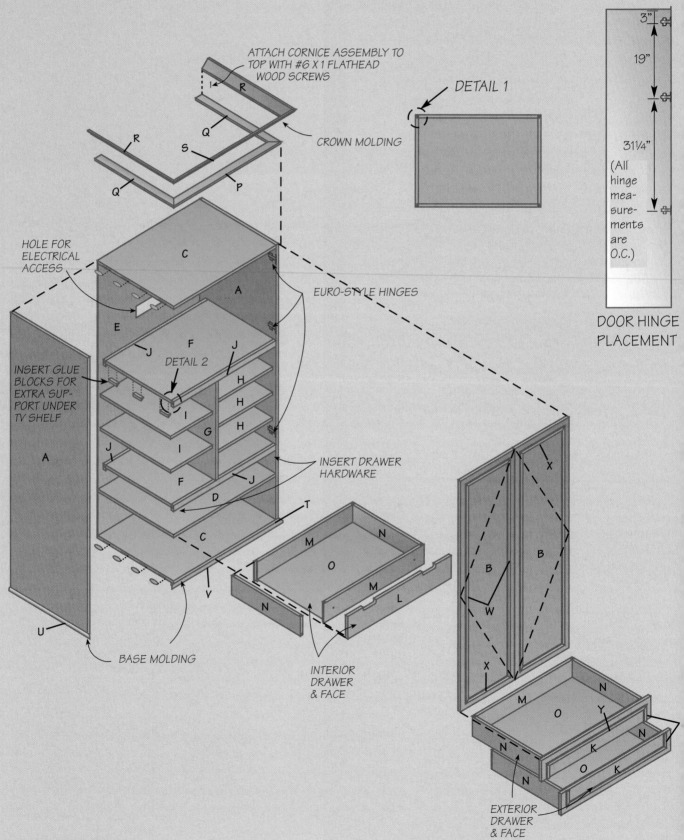

ATTACH CORNICE ASSEMBLY TO TOP WITH #6 X 1 FLATHEAD WOOD SCREWS

CROWN MOLDING

DETAIL 1

3"
19"
31¼"
(All hinge mea-sure-ments are O.C.)

DOOR HINGE PLACEMENT

HOLE FOR ELECTRICAL ACCESS

EURO-STYLE HINGES

DETAIL 2

INSERT GLUE BLOCKS FOR EXTRA SUP-PORT UNDER TV SHELF

INSERT DRAWER HARDWARE

BASE MOLDING

INTERIOR DRAWER & FACE

EXTERIOR DRAWER & FACE

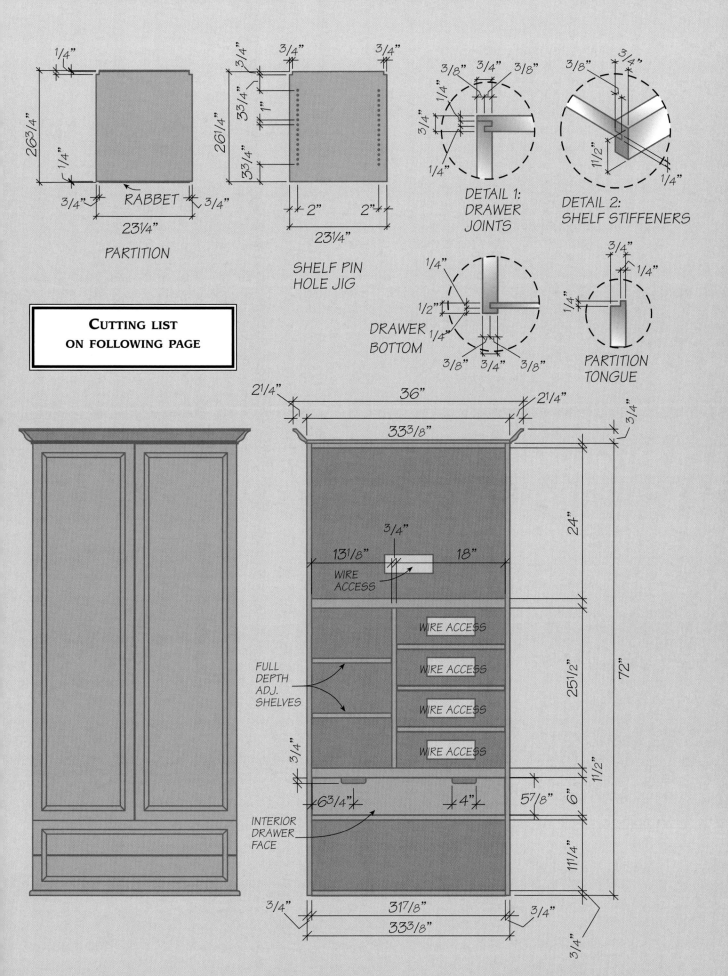

1/4"

26¾"

1/4"

3/4"   RABBET   3/4"

23¼"

PARTITION

3/4"

3/4"   3/4"

33¾"

1"

26¼"

33¾"

2"   2"

23¼"

SHELF PIN
HOLE JIG

3/8"   3/4"   3/8"

1/4"

3/4"

1/4"

DETAIL 1:
DRAWER
JOINTS

3/8"   3/4"

1½"

1/4"

DETAIL 2:
SHELF STIFFENERS

1/4"

1/2"

1/4"

3/8"   3/4"   3/8"

DRAWER
BOTTOM

3/4"

1/4"

1/4"

1/4"

PARTITION
TONGUE

CUTTING LIST
ON FOLLOWING PAGE

2¼"   36"   2¼"

33⅜"

3/4"

24"

3/4"

13⅛"   18"

WIRE
ACCESS

WIRE ACCESS

WIRE ACCESS

25½"   72"

FULL
DEPTH
ADJ.
SHELVES

WIRE ACCESS

WIRE ACCESS

3/4"

1½"

6¾"   4"

57/8"   6"

INTERIOR
DRAWER
FACE

11¼"

3/4"   31⅞"   3/4"

33⅜"

3/4"

Armoire Cutting List

Part	No.	Size	Material
CARCASE			
A. Sides	2	¾ × 23⅝ × 72"	Oak Plywood
B. Doors	2	¾ × 16⅝ × 59⅞"	"
C. Top, Floor	2	¾ × 23⅝ × 31⅞"	"
D. Bottom Shelf	1	¾ × 23⅝ × 31⅞"	"
E. Back	1	¼ × 32½ × 71"*	Lauan Plywood

*Cut to size after assembling carcase

Part	No.	Size	Material
TV/COMPONENT SHELF PARTS			
F. TV Shelf/ Components Shelf	2	¾ × 21¼ × 31⅞"	Oak Plywood
G. Partition	1	¾ × 23¼ × 26¾*	"
H. Adjustable Shelves	3	¾ × 17⅞" × 23⅛"**	"
I. Adjustable Shelves	2	¾ × 13 × 23⅛"**	"

*Measure and cut to length after carcase is assembled. See text.
**Cut these parts to size AFTER the partition is installed. See text.

Part	No.	Size	Material
SOLID-WOOD EDGING			
J. Shelf Edging	4	¾ × 1½ × 31⅞"	Oak
DRAWERS			
K. Exterior Drawer Faces	2	¾ × 5½ × 33⁵⁄₁₆"	Oak Plywood
L. Interior Drawer Face	1	¾ × 5⅞ × 31¹¹⁄₁₆"**	"
M. Drawer Fronts/Backs	6	¾ × 5 × 30⅞"	"
N. Drawer Sides	6	¾ × 5 × 21½"	"
O. Drawer bottoms	3	¼ × 21 × 30⅛"	Lauan Plywood

*Install edging on sides first, then make cove cuts (hand grips). If desired, edge the cove with glue-on veneer edging.
**Install edging on top edge; form edging into hand-hold cutouts with heat gun to melt glue, then press in with block of wood.

Part	No.	Size	Material
MOLDINGS			
P. Cornice Cleat	1	½ × 2 × 33⅜"	Pine
Q. Cornice Cleats	2	½ × 2 × 24⅝"	"
R. Cornice	2	½ × 2¼ × 26⅞"	Oak
S. Cornice	1	½ × 2¼ × 36"*	"
T. Base Cleat	1	¾ × ¾ × 33⅜"	"
U. Shoe (Base)	2	¾ × ¾ × 25⅛"	"
V. Shoe (Base)	1	¾ × ¾ × 34⅜"**	"
W. Door Molding	4	¼ × 1¼ × 56⅞"	"
X. Door Molding	4	¼ × 1¼ × 13⅝"***	"
Y. Drawer Molding	2	¼ × 1¼ × 30⅜"	"
Z. Drawer Molding	2	¼ × 1¼ × 8⅜"****	"

*   Cut to length after Cornice R pieces are installed
**   Cut to length after Shoe Base T piece is installed
*** Cut to length after Door Molding W pieces are installed
****Cut 8⅜-in. strips in two pieces after marking location where drawers meet

Cutting Layouts

¼" Lauan Plywood

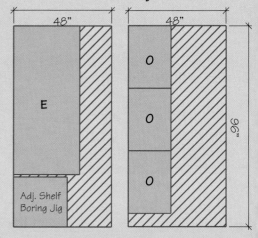

¾" Oak Plywood

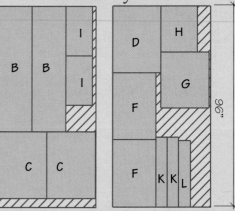

¾" Oak Plywood

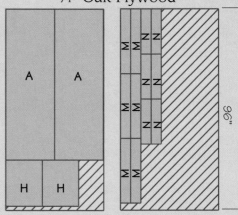

FIGURE B: Glue and clamp shelf stiffeners to the front edges of the TV and component shelves. Dry fit the back stiffeners into place—they'll protect the back edge rabbets from getting crushed by the clamps.

Cut the carcase & shelf parts

1 Begin by laying out all the carcase and shelf parts on ¾-in. oak plywood (See *Cutting Layout,* page 96). We've arranged the parts to best utilize four 4 × 8 plywood sheets. However, be sure to lay out the TV and component shelves side-by-side, as illustrated in the *Cutting Layout.* You'll cut a dado across both of these shelves (See step 3, below) before they're separated. This will ensure that the dadoes will line up exactly in the armoire carcase.

2 Cut the sides, top, floor panel, and bottom shelf to size, but do not cut the TV and component shelves apart.

3 Cut one long ¼-in.- × ¼-in. dado in the piece you reserved for the TV and component shelves,

FIGURE A: Gang-rout one long dado in the panel you've reserved for the TV and component shelf before separating the shelves from one another. This will ensure that the dadoes line up perfectly in the carcase when you assemble it.

using a router and a straightedge guide (**See FIGURE A**). Alternately you could cut the groove on a table saw with a dado set (See *Dado-blade sets,* page 27) with the table saw fence set 18 in. from the blade. Then rip-cut the TV and component shelves to width.

4 Rout the ¼-in.-deep × ⅜-in.-wide rabbet along the inside back edge of the top, floor and side pieces of the carcase using a piloted rabbeting bit. This will enable the back of the carcase to set into the sides.

Install the shelf stiffeners

1 Cut the solid-oak stiffeners for the TV and component shelves to size. Plow the ¼-in. × ⅜-in. groove in the stiffeners with a dado set in the table saw (See page 27), then cut the rabbet in the back and front edges of the TV and component shelves using a router and either a piloted rabbet bit or a straight bit and edge guide.

2 Glue shelf stiffeners to the front rabbets of the TV and component shelves (**See FIGURE B**). NOTE: Orient the stiffeners on both shelf rabbets so the top edge of the stiffener is flush with the top side of each shelf. The back-edge stiffeners will be glued into position later. For now, dry-fit the back stiffeners into their rabbets when you clamp the front stiffeners; the back stiffeners will protect the rabbets on the back edge of the shelves from getting crushed by the clamps.

FIGURE C: Enlist the help of a buddy or two when you glue up the armoire carcase. Pull the biscuit joints tight between the sides, shelves, and top and bottom pieces with clamps and cauls that stretch the width of the sides. Clamping will go much more smoothly if you glue up the carcase on top of sawhorses—this way the floor won't interfere with the clamp heads or pipes.

FIGURE D: Apply self-adhesive veneer tape to the exposed edges of the plywood using a household iron to activate the adhesive. The tin foil distributes heat more evenly and protects the iron from glue.

Assemble the carcase

1 Lay out with pencil and straightedge the position of each fixed shelf on the inside face of both armoire sides. Do this by laying the sides flat with the inside faces up and top and bottom edges aligned. Mark each shelf position across both faces at once.

2 Dry-assemble and clamp the carcase with the fixed horizontal members— top, shelves and floor panel—in position and the carcase laying on its back. All of the fixed horizontal members will attach to the armoire sides with four #20 biscuits spaced equally from the front of the carcase to the back. Mark the position of each biscuit with a pencil line on both members of each joint (See *Biscuit joints,* page 106). Label all of the carcase parts clearly to avoid confusion during glue-up, then unclamp the carcase and cut the biscuit slots.

3 Dry-fit the carcase together again, checking the fit of each biscuit in its slot. Don't underestimate how tricky this maneuver will be; an extra helper or two will be essential during glue-up. Prepare for glue-up by laying one carcase side on sawhorses with the biscuit slots facing up. Spread glue into the biscuit slots of this side and then across the corresponding edges of the horizontal members. Slide the biscuits into their slots in the side piece, and set the shelves, top, and floor panel on-end onto the biscuits. If you avoid unnecessary jarring, they should stand on their own without further support.

4 Spread glue across the other edges and slots of the shelves, top, and floor panel, and slide these biscuits in. Lay the other side piece on top of the carcase assembly and maneuver the side into place. Biscuits expand as the glue soaks into them, but you should have plenty of time to fit the carcase together before this becomes a problem.

5 Clamp the carcase at each joint with an even number of clamps front and back, and protect the outside faces of the carcase with wood cauls (See **FIGURE C**). Since the center of the carcase can't be pulled together directly with clamps, use cauls long enough to span the width of the sides so the cauls, clamped on either end, can help press the center of each joint snug. Be sure to keep the

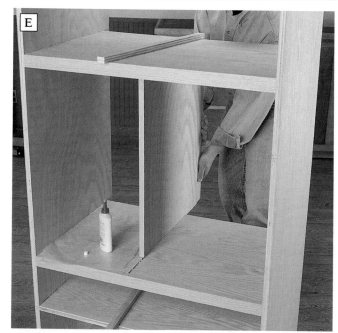

FIGURE E: Spread glue into the component-shelf dado and along the top rabbet of the vertical partition, then slide the partition into place. Be sure to notch the partition's bottom corner first, so it will fit over the shelf stiffener.

FIGURE F: Rip-cut and cross-cut triangular blocks from scrap stock. Then glue four along the length of each shelf to reinforce the biscuit joints. No metal fasteners are needed. Wipe up excess glue with a damp cloth before the glue dries.

front edges of the horizontal members flush with the front edges of the sides.

6 Square the carcase by measuring the diagonals and adjusting the clamps as needed. Wipe up glue drips with damp shop rags. Then do not disturb the carcase until the glue dries.

7 Apply iron-on edging to the front carcase edges (See **FIGURE D** and *Iron-on edge banding,* page 112) and trim off the excess with a sharp utility knife or edge-band trimming tool.

Cut & install the vertical partition

1 Determine the length of the vertical partition by measuring the distance between the TV and component shelves where they join one side of the carcase. Add the depth of the dadoes (½ in. total) to this length. (NOTE: If we were to determine the partition's length by measuring the actual distance between the shelf dadoes, it wouldn't account for the possibility that the shelves might be slightly bowed in the carcase.)

2 Cut the partition to length, then cut ¼-in. × ¼-in. rabbets on the top and bottom edges with a router, just as you rabbeted the TV and component shelves. Apply iron-on edging to the partition's front edge and remove any excess edging.

3 Test-fit the partition in the carcase (**See FIGURE E**), then mark and cut out the ¾-in. × 1-in. notches from the partition's corners so it will fit over the front and back shelf stiffeners and be flush with the carcase front.

4 Glue in the partition. Use bar clamps and wood cauls to pull the partition tight to the TV and component shelves. This will flatten any bowing that might be present in the shelves.

5 Glue and clamp the solid-wood stiffeners into the rabbet grooves on the back edges of the TV and component shelves.

Build the adjustable shelves & rout pin recesses

1 Make a ¼-in. plywood shelf pin jig (page 105) to use as a guide for drilling the adjustable-shelf pin holes. The pin holes go all the way through the partition, so use a backer board to keep your drill bit from tearing out the plywood when it penetrates through the other side. Cut the dowel pins that will support the adjustable shelves.

2 Measure and cut the adjustable plywood shelves to size and cover the front edges of the shelves with iron-on edging.

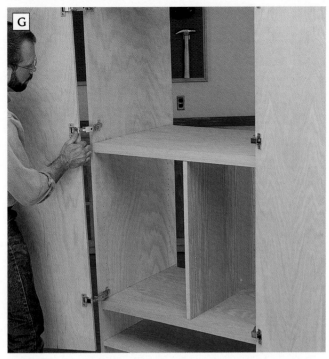

FIGURE G: Once you've attached the concealed hinge hardware to the insides of the carcase and doors, slide the hinge components together to hang the doors. Then use the three adjustment screws on each hinge to move the doors into final position so they're square with the carcase and hang evenly with one another.

3 Insert four dowel pins into the carcase and use them as references for marking the locations of the dowel pin recesses that you'll cut in the bottom of each shelf (these are simply grooves cut into the undersides of the shelves to house the dowel pins, preventing the shelf from rolling). Cut the recesses with a router and straight bit.

Reinforce the butt joints

1 On the table saw, miter-cut and rip-cut 1 × 1 pine into triangular glue blocks that are 2 in. long. These will reinforce each biscuit joint from below in all horizontal members except the floor panel. Apply glue liberally to the square side of each glue block and slide it back and forth in place until it grabs (See FIGURE F, page 99). Space four blocks evenly over the length of each joint. No nails are necessary.

Install the hinges, doors & latches

1 Measure and cut the doors to size and conceal the plywood edges with iron-on edging. Trim off the excess.

2 Lay out the hinge and base plate locations (See Concealed hinges, page 111) for three hinges spaced down from the top of the door. Placement

of these parts is critical for the hinge to operate properly, so follow the manufacturer's instructions carefully.

3 Bore the large hinge recesses in the backs of the doors on a drill press using the size Forstner bit recommended by the hinge manufacturer. Screw the base plates to the insides of the cabinet, attach the hinge hardware to the doors, and snap the hinges onto the baseplates (See FIGURE G) to hang the doors. Tweak the three-way adjustable base plate screws to align the doors so they're even with one another when closed and square in the carcase.

4 Install push latches to the door backs and inside the carcase according to the manufacturer's instructions. Adjust as necessary until the doors close and latch flush with one another.

Build the drawers

1 Measure the carcase openings for the three drawers, then cut the plywood drawer sides, fronts, and backs to size (See Cutting list, page 96). Also cut two test pieces the same width and thickness as a drawer side and front or back.

2 Cut a dado in the test piece that represents the front or back, following the dimensions shown in the diagram on page 95. Center the dado groove on the edge. Adjust the set-up if needed and cut the

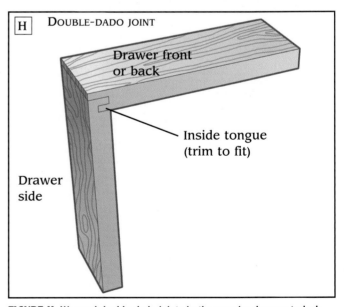

FIGURE H: We used double-dado joints in the armoire drawers to lock the front and back of each drawer to the sides. The joints are easy to construct on the table saw. Cut grooves into each member of the joint, then trim the inside tongue of the dado on the front and back drawer pieces until the joint slides together.

groove in the front and back pieces of each drawer. This groove forms half of the double-dado joint that locks the drawer boxes together **(See FIGURE H)**. Also see **FIGURE I** for a diagram of how drawers of this type fit together.

3 Cut dadoes in each end of each drawer side. Complete the double-dado joint by removing slightly less than one-half the length of the inside tongue of the dadoes on the drawer front and back pieces. Dry-fit the front and back of each drawer to the sides and check the fit. The aim is for each double-dado joint to lock fully together. Trim the inside tongues until each joint fits tightly.

4 Cut the drawer bottom grooves in each drawer part, using a table saw equipped with a dado blade or with a router guided by a fence.

5 Dry-fit the drawer boxes again and measure for the drawer bottoms. Cut the bottoms to size from ¼-in. lauan plywood. Spread glue into the two grooves of each double dado and assemble the three drawers with clamps and cauls. The drawer bottoms can "float" freely in their grooves without glue. Check for drawer squareness by measuring the diagonals and reclamp if necessary.

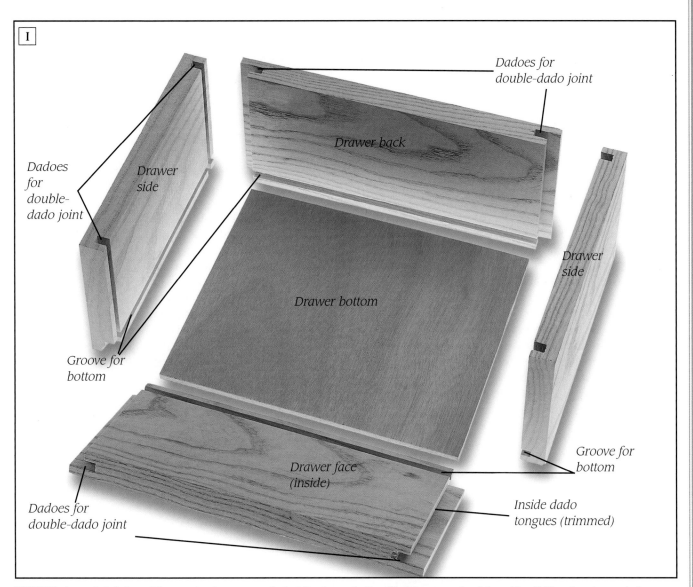

I

Dadoes for double-dado joint

Dadoes for double-dado joint

Drawer side

Drawer back

Drawer side

Groove for bottom

Drawer bottom

Groove for bottom

Dadoes for double-dado joint

Drawer face (inside)

Inside dado tongues (trimmed)

FIGURE I: An exploded view of the armoire drawers reveals that the drawer bottom fits into a grove in all four sides. Unlike other drawer designs, where the bottom slides in last and gets nailed into place on the bottom of the drawer back, the bottom in a drawer with double-dado joints is held captive by all four sides without fasteners. Double dadoes are a good choice for larger drawers because the joints lock together and resist racking.

FIGURE J: Telescoping metal slides on the armoire drawers allow the drawers to open to their full depth without falling out. These are a good choice for deep drawers because the contents in back of the drawer remain fully accessible.

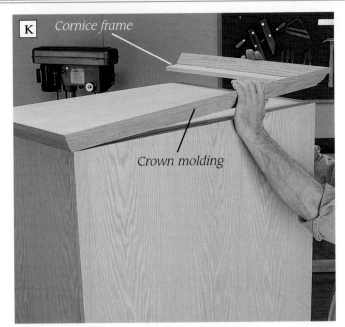

Cornice frame

Crown molding

FIGURE K: Assemble the cornice frame, then nail the crown molding to it before attaching it to the top of the armoire carcase. This way, you can build the whole cornice at a comfortable working height before screwing it into place.

Hang the drawers

1 Measure and attach the metal drawer slide hardware with screws (See *Metal drawer slides*, page 109) to the inside of the armoire carcase and the drawer sides. Then install the drawers (**See FIGURE J**). Adjust the drawer slides until the drawers hang neatly in the openings and are square with the front of the carcase.

2 Cut the three false drawer faces, then cut the hand-holds into the top of the interior drawer face: lay out and rout shallow cove-shaped hand grips in the sides of the exterior drawer (the drawers below the doors) faces. Edge the drawer faces with iron-on tape, trim off the excess, then install the drawer faces with glue and screws.

Build the cornice

1 Cut and assemble the cornice frame with glue and nails. The corners of the frame are mitered at 45°. Note that the finished cornice frame is longer than the armoire top. It will overhang the carcase so it can sit flush with the front edge of the doors.

2 Cut a piece of crown molding at 45° to cap one of the armoire sides using a miter box and a back saw. You can also use a power miter saw and a crown-molding jig to complete these compound miter cuts. Attach the crown side piece to the cor-

nice frame with glue and finishing nails. Repeat for the other side cornice piece.

3 Measure and cut the front cornice piece. Attach it to the cornice frame and both crown molding sides with glue and finishing nails. Set the nails below the surface and use oak-colored putty to fill the nail holes on all three sides.

4 Sand the cornice assembly and lay it on top of the armoire (**See FIGURE K**). Adjust it for the front overhang and install it by screwing the cornice frame to the armoire top.

Attach the molding

1 Lay out with pencil and square the location where the trim molding will go on the faces of the doors and drawers. The outline you create will act as a frame for tacking the molding into place.

2 Cut one piece of molding at a time, mitering the corners at 45°. Fit and tack each successive piece as you go, using ¾-in. brads (leave the heads above the surface of the molding for easy removal). Once all the pieces are fit in place, remove the molding, pull the brads, and glue and nail it back into place with finishing nails. Set the nailheads below the surface (**See FIGURE L**) and cover the holes with putty.

FIGURE M: Measure the shelf spacing and transfer the positions of major components to the back panel so you can cut access slots.

FIGURE L: Tack the trim molding one piece at a time to the doors and drawers, following outlines you've pencilled onto the surfaces. Once all the pieces fit properly, glue and nail each piece into place.

3 Cut and install the baseshoe cleat to the front of the floor piece with glue and finishing nails. Miter-cut and attach the baseshoe molding to the front cleat. Then, cut and attach the base-shoe side pieces. Set all the nails below the wood surface and fill with putty.

Install the back panel

1 Measure the opening and cut the back to size. Position the back panel near the rabbeted opening it fits into, and make rough marks for access slots **(See FIGURE M).** The access slots should correspond to the positioning of your electronic components. Cut access slots in the back panel with a jig saw.

2 Install the back with glue and brads—we used a pneumatic nailer **(See FIGURE N).**

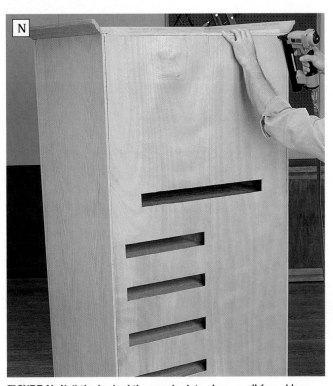

FIGURE N: Nail the back of the armoire into place on all four sides— we used a pneumatic pin nailer. No glue is necessary.

Finishing touches

Sand the entire cabinet with 150-, 180-, then 220-grit sandpaper. Apply the stain of your choice and wipe off any excess with a clean cloth before the stain dries. Let the stain dry. Apply two coats of polyurethane varnish, sanding with 400-grit paper between coats. TIP: If the floors in your home are uneven, attach adjustable furniture glides to the bottom of the entertainment center.

Shelf stiffeners

1 Cut dado grooves in each shelf stiffener using a dado-blade set in the table saw (See page 27). Position the dado on the stiffener so it will cap the front of the shelf evenly with the shelf's top surface. If the dado is cut too low, the stiffener will form a lip on the front of the shelf rather than sitting flush.

2 Cut rabbets on the front and back edges of the shelf to match the depth and thickness of the stiffener dadoes. If you cut the rabbets with a dado set, be sure to use a wooden auxiliary fence so the blades won't cut into the metal saw fence.

WOODWORKING SKILLS
Making shelves with shelf stiffeners

Shelf stiffeners are wood strips installed on the front and back edges of wide shelves to keep them from bowing under weight. Stiffeners also serve a decorative function on plywood shelves because they hide laminations and voids and give the shelves a more substantial appearance.

Stiffeners can be attached simply with glue and nails. A stronger method, however, is to dado the back face of the stiffener and cut a rabbet along the edge of the shelf to fit the dado. This way the stiffener locks into the shelf and provides maximum span strength.

To stiffen the shelves in this fashion, cut the dado groove in the back face of the stiffeners on the table saw. Clamp a featherboard to the table to keep the workpiece flush against the saw fence, and keep a push stick handy. You can also cut the dado with a straight bit in a router equipped with an edge guide.

Cut a rabbet to match the stiffener dado along the front and back edge of the shelf. Since the rabbets must be cut on the edges of the shelf, be sure to use an auxiliary fence on the table saw to keep the dado from scoring your metal saw fence. Cut the rabbets on a test piece first and adjust the fit before edging your shelves.

3 Glue and clamp the stiffeners to the shelves. Use wood cauls between the stiffeners and the clamp heads to distribute the clamping pressure and to keep from marring the stiffener faces. If you need to glue on one stiffener at a time, dry fit the other one in place and use it to protect the rabbet from clamping pressure.

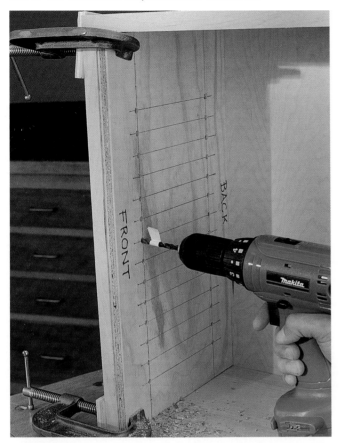

1 Bore holes for adjustable shelf pins by first clamping your shop-made jig into position. It should fit the area where the shelves will go. Then mark the drilling depth on the bit with tape. Drill each hole, holding the drill perpendicular to the jig.

Installing adjustable shelves

Adjustable shelves are a great way to expand the shelving flexibility of a cabinet. The downside is that dowel pins won't hold the shelves in place, should the cabinet get jarred. An easy way to remedy this problem is to cut notches into the underside of the shelf for the pins, which will keep it from sliding.

You can bore the adjustable shelf holes using perforated hardboard (See *TIP,* page 22), or you can make your own template with a piece of ¾-in. plywood. To use the latter method, cut a piece of plywood that fits into the opening where the shelves will go, then use a marking gauge or combination square to draw a vertical line 1 in. from the front edge of the jig and 2½ in. from the back. Then use a square to draw horizontal lines at 1-in. intervals across the jig. Bore shelf pin holes at each intersection to match the diameter of the dowels you plan to use.

Mark the jig "front" and "back" on both faces, and clamp the jig in the cabinet. Bore perpendicular holes with a hand-held drill, making sure not to bore through the outside of the cabinet. Move and clamp the jig to the other side, keeping the jig in the same orientation—this way even if you've bored some holes off center in the jig, the holes will align.

Now, insert four shelf pins, set a shelf in place, and mark the pin locations on the bottom of the shelf. Use a router and a straight bit that matches the diameter of the shelf pins to rout a notch the length and thickness of the pins.

2 Install four pins and set a shelf into position. Pencil an outline around each pin on the bottom of the shelf. These will serve as guides for routing the notched recesses.

3 Install a straight bit that matches or slightly exceeds the diameter of the shelf pins in your router. Set the depth of cut to match the diameter of the pins and rout each notch. We show routing the notches freehand, but you may want to use a fence to guide the cuts.

Making biscuit joints

Biscuit joints (also called plate joints) are a quick and efficient method for joining sheet goods, as well as for joining solid boards. They work on either butted edges or edge-to-face applications to form butt joints, corner joints, edge-glued joints, and more. The completed joint is actually stronger than those reinforced with most conventional fasteners.

The biscuit joiner is equipped with a small blade that plunges semicircular slots into each member of a joint. The fence on the front of the tool adjusts according to the size of the biscuit that will be inserted; and it also sets the angle and the position of the slot on the board.

Biscuits, which lock the joint together, are football-shaped disks made of compressed wood. When they come into contact with wet glue, the moisture expands them into the slots, tightening the joint. They come in several standard sizes (#0, which is ⅜ in. × 1¼ in.; #10, which is ¾ in. × 2⅛ in.; and #20, which is 1 in. × 2⅜ in.) to cover a range of joint applications.

Building a biscuit joint is easy, no matter what kind of joint you're reinforcing. The basic strategy is to dry-fit the parts together, then draw a line across both mating parts to mark the center of the slot the biscuit will fit into. From there, you simply align the

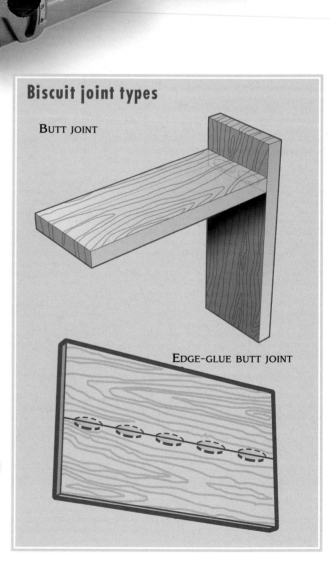

Biscuit joint types

BUTT JOINT

EDGE-GLUE BUTT JOINT

STANDARD BISCUIT SIZES
(SHOWN ACTUAL SIZE)

fence on the biscuit joiner with each mark (after disassembling the dry-assembly) and cut slots for the biscuits. The tool automatically creates uniform setbacks and slot sizes.

Then, simply apply glue to a biscuit that matches the size of the slots, insert the biscuit into one of the mating parts, then make the joint.

Before making a cut with a biscuit joiner, make sure that the workpiece is secured to your worksurface—about the only way to botch up a biscuit cut is to have the workpiece shift as you engage it with the biscuit blade. To keep the tool itself from slipping, most have an anti-slip device (either a rubber tip or a metal point) to help maintain the grip on the wood.

HOW TO ASSEMBLE A CARCASE WITH BISCUIT JOINTS

1 Dry-assemble the carcase and mark the plate locations directly onto the parts of the assembly. Draw straight lines across the joints at 6- to 8-in. intervals, using a combination square or a try square as a guide.

2 Disassemble the dry-assembly, then cut the biscuit slots. Align the reference marks you've drawn with the permanent alignment mark on the biscuit joiner and press the joiner into the edge of the boards to engage the blade and cut the slots.

3 To cut the slots for the shelves, first mark the side panels at the planned shelf locations. Position the shelf on the mark, with the shelf edges flush with the side edges. Mark the plate locations and cut the slots in the shelf edges.

CONTINUED NEXT PAGE

4 Keeping the shelf in place, make the slots in the side. Reposition the shelf on the other side and repeat.

5 With all the slots cut, you're ready for assembly. Lay both sides edge-to-edge, inside face up, and apply glue into the slots and on the mating surfaces. Insert the plates in the sides, then lay in the top, floor and shelves one at a time.

6 Glue-up the assembly with clamps and wood cauls that apply pressure along the length of the joint. Squaring the assembly is particularly important when doors and drawers will be installed. Neither will operate properly in an out-of-square unit. Carefully check for square by measuring the diagonals.

HOW TO HANG DRAWERS WITH METAL SLIDES

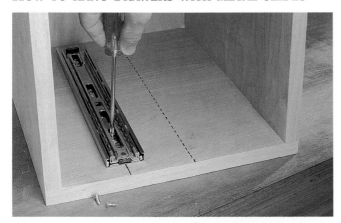

1 Carefully measure from a reference point—a fixed shelf, for example—to the center of the drawer location in the opening. Use a square to draw a line parallel to the shelf. Align the slide's mounting holes with the line and mark the slotted (adjustable) holes.

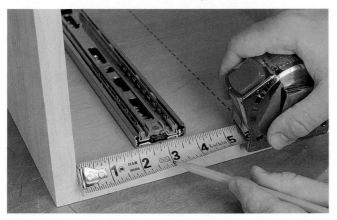

2 Drive screws through the slotted holes and into the cabinet side to mount the slide. Repeat to install the slide on the opposite side. Measure from the top of the drawer opening to the midpoint of the slide. Subtract ⅛ in. and measure down that amount from the top of the drawer. Mark lines on each side of the drawer at this point.

3 Attach the rails to the drawer sides, centered on the reference lines. Make sure the rails don't extend past the drawer front or back.

Hanging drawers with metal slides

The most finely crafted drawer in existence will eventually cause you some headaches if you install it without a drawer slide. A drawer slide can be anything from a home-made set of hardwood cleats to a highly engineered, top-of-line metal slide with lubricated bearings and other high-tech features. For most woodworking projects with drawers, an ordinary side-mount metal slide is more than adequate.

The installation procedure for hanging drawers with metal slides varies somewhat between styles and manufacturers. Obviously, a drawer slide that mounts beneath the door is installed quite differently than a side-mount version. But most metal slides are two-part assemblies: one part (the slide) mounts to the cabinet, and the other part (the rail) is attached to the drawer.

The drawer slide shown here is a mid-price, two-piece full-extension metal drawer slide system. The slide rail is a single piece that's installed on the drawer; the second piece consists of three separate parts that open like a telescope, allowing the drawer to travel the entire rail length. (Standard slides stop several inches before the end of the slide rail.) Full-extension slides are available in 10- to 24-in. lengths, sold by 2-in. increments. Like most metal slides, they can be adjusted for a precise fit even after the parts are installed.

4 Test the fit by mounting the drawer rails inside the slides. If necessary, adjust the slides by moving them up or down on the slotted holes until the drawer fits squarely in the opening, then install screws in the fixed holes.

Armoire Entertainment Center 109

Metal drawer slides

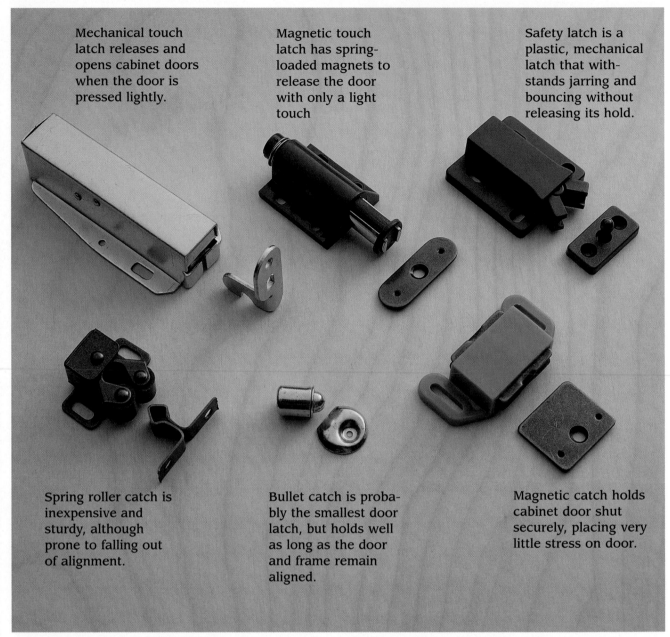

Mechanical touch latch releases and opens cabinet doors when the door is pressed lightly.

Magnetic touch latch has spring-loaded magnets to release the door with only a light touch

Safety latch is a plastic, mechanical latch that with-stands jarring and bouncing without releasing its hold.

Spring roller catch is inexpensive and sturdy, although prone to falling out of alignment.

Bullet catch is proba-bly the smallest door latch, but holds well as long as the door and frame remain aligned.

Magnetic catch holds cabinet door shut securely, placing very little stress on door.

A variety of latch options are available for holding cabinet doors closed. The ones we show here each consist of two parts: a plate that attaches to the inside of the door with one or two screws and a catch that mounts to the inside of the cabinet carcase. Each type functions a little differently. Some latch by means of spring-loaded rollers or pauls that snap around a protrusion on the plate. Others hold the door closed when a spring-loaded pin locks into an indentation on the door plate. Still others use magnets that align with and attract the plate to draw the cabinet door tight.

WOODWORKING SKILLS:
Cabinet latches

Cabinet latches fall into two basic categories: *mechanical latches* and *magnetic latches*. Mechanical latches generally use tempered steel or another springy material that flexes under pressure to fit into or around a fixed receptacle. Magnetic latches usually have magnets in the barrel of the latch that clamp onto the metal strike plate mounted on the door. Selecting latches for your cabinet or casework is mostly a matter of personal preference, budget and style. Also consider the difficulty of installation—some latches require mortising or drilling, which can be a lot trickier than simple surface-mount hardware.

WOODWORKING SKILLS

Hanging cabinet doors with concealed hinges

Concealed hinges offer many advantages, but ease of installation is not one of them. Still, these European-style hinges are durable, smooth-operating and they stay hidden from view when the doors are closed. You can also find concealed hinges with unusually wide swing radii—like the model shown here, which opens up a full 165°.

Concealed hinges consist of an adjustable metal base plate, installed inside the cabinet, and the hinge itself, which is installed on the door. You'll need a drill press and a 35mm Forstner-type drill bit to install the hinges. Be sure to read the manufacturer's instructions before installing concealed hinges. The specific techniques vary quite a bit, and many have restrictive placement limitations.

HOW TO INSTALL CONCEALED HINGES

1 Mark the centerpoint for the round hinge mortises on the cabinet door, following the manufacturer's spacing directions.

2 Drill the round mortises at the centerpoints with a Forstner bit and drill press. Many concealed hinges are installed with a 35 mm bit.

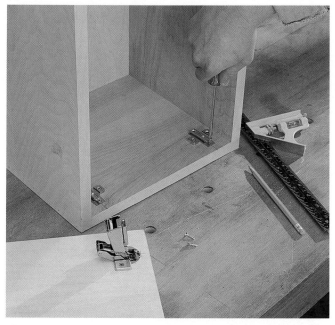

3 Measure and mark the base-plate locations on the cabinet sides, then screw the base plates in position.

4 Slide the door hinges onto the base plates and screw them into place. The base plates allow you to adjust the door in six directions: in, out, up, down, left and right. Work the adjusting screws until the doors are flush on top and bottom, with an even gap between the doors. See page 90 for a view of these hinges in action.

IRON-ON EDGE BANDING

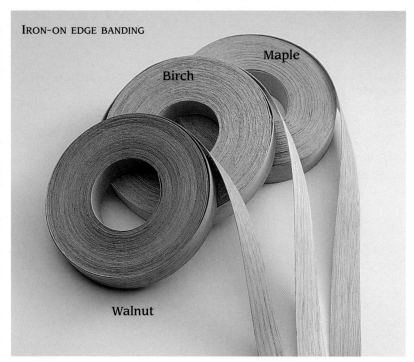

Maple

Birch

Walnut

Iron-on veneer edge banding is quick and relatively easy to attach to the exposed edges of plywood for a more finished appearance. The strips, usually sold in rolls, are backed with heat-activated glue that bonds to the plywood edge when it's passed over with a hot iron. Banding made from a few selected wood species is widely available at woodworking stores and even building centers, but for more exotic edging you'll probably need to look into thin strips of unbacked veneer.

WOODWORKING SKILLS
Applying iron-on edge banding

Plywood edges occasionally are left exposed for decorative effect. But in most cases they're covered, usually with the same wood species as the face veneer. You can cut your own edging from solid wood, or you can cover plywood edges with prefabricated edge veneer tape, or edge banding, which comes in 50-foot rolls. It's also available in 8-foot lengths for small projects, and 250-foot rolls for heavy users. The edging is $13/16$ in. wide (it also comes in 1 in. and 2 in. widths), which is wide enough to completely cover $3/4$-in.-thick plywood edges with some overhang.

There are two types of edging rolls: iron-on edging, which is backed by an adhesive that's activated under heat, and glue-on edging, which is backed with paper and glued down with contact cement applied both to the plywood edge and to the backside of the edging. Iron-on edging is less messy to work with and is our preferred type.

HOW TO APPLY IRON-ON EDGE BANDING

1 Begin by cutting the edging for vertical surfaces to length with a utility knife. Cut the pieces slightly over-long.

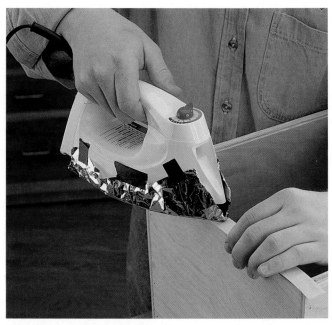

2 Cover the foot of an ordinary household iron with tin foil to protect the iron from the glue. Set the iron to a low heat setting, and allow it to warm up. With the veneer strip in position, press it with the iron, moving gradually forward away from one corner. The tape should completely cover the plywood edge, but try to hug the inside edge of the workpiece so there's less overhang on the inside of the project.

3 To guarantee a good glue bond, roll the edge banding with a wall-paper seam roller after each piece is applied. Try to work the roller in one direction only in case there are any trapped air bubbles.

4 Once the vertical pieces are applied, measure the horizontal pieces for the top, bottom and fixed shelves. Cut these pieces to exact length using a square to guide the cut.

Edge-banding Trimmer

5 When all the pieces are applied and rolled, trim the overhang. Work in the same direction as the grain to avoid tearing the edging. We used a special edge-banding trimmer (See inset photo), which is virtually fool-proof. But you can also get a nice clean trim line with a cabinet scraper or even a sharp utility knife.

Armoire Entertainment Center 113

Garden Bench

Add a touch of style and comfort to your outdoor living with this elegant garden bench. The graceful lines of the slats and the minimal ornamentation allow the beauty of white oak, one of the original outdoor woods, to shine through. And if you appreciate creative joinery, you'll love learning how this beautiful bench fits together.

Woodworking Skills You'll Learn:

- Constructing dowel-pinned, half-lap joints

- Basics of bench design

- Measuring and cutting crisp through-mortises

- Selecting outdoor woods and wood finishes

• Cutting lap joint dadoes with a router

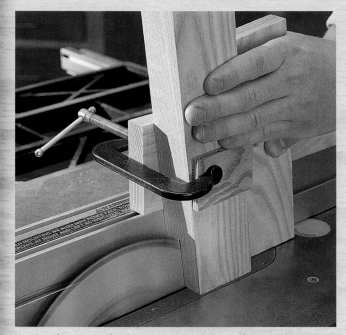

• Cutting angled tenons with a jig

• Transferring patterns to a workpiece

• Making wedged mortise-and-tenon joints

Design Features

Doweled half-lap through T joint

Contoured arms

Angled rear legs

Top back rail

Back slats with diamond cutouts

Bottom back rail

Seat slats

Side seat rail

Front seat rail

Front leg

Lower rail

Through-wedged tenons

Doweled modified part-blind half-lap T joints

Doweled modified through half-lap T joints

Garden Bench

The garden bench originated in England, famous for its formal gardens. Most garden benches span about 60 inches across. At 54 inches wide, our downsized bench is very comfortable for two people. Built with white oak, the bench is constructed primarily with doweled lap joints and a mortise-tenon joint that's strengthened with the wedges. The only metal fasteners found on this bench are the brass screws used to attach the seat slats to the seat rails.

Material

There are a number of woods that can withstand the elements, making them suitable for outdoor furniture. Perhaps the most well known outdoor wood is teak, a favorite of boat builders. Teak has natural oils that allow it to withstand weather and protect it from attack by insects. However, these same oils also resist glue, and teak joints must be wiped with a solvent such as MEK (methyl ethyl ketone) to dissolve the oils prior to gluing. There are many other outdoor woods, but the hardness, durability and tight grain of white oak make it our choice for the bench.

Outdoor woods & finishes

Naturally weather-resistant woods include, from left to right, redwood, cedar, white oak and teak.

Extra protection for wood exposed to the elements can be found with wood sealer (left) and exterior spar varnish (right).

Design

For a bench to support a heavy load, the legs must be sturdy and the rails that support the seat slats must be attached with strong joints. In addition, the seat should be shaped to conform to the human figure and the back rest should be angled for comfort. These are the main factors in considering the bench proportions, dimensions and shape.

The seat height is lower than the seat height of a typical chair because chairs, such as the side chair in Chapter 3, generally are designed to be used at a table. A lower seat is more conducive to relaxed posture. The seat depth is similar to the depth on a traditional chair. The seat arms are scooped, also for comfort. The ends of the seat arms are rounded over, and the tops of the rear legs are rounded to mimic the front ends of the arms. The diamond cutouts in the back slats are decorative.

Materials & construction

Perhaps the biggest disadvantage to using white oak is the tannin in oak. When moisture and steel come into contact with oak, it reacts with the tannin, often causing a black stain. For that reason, and to remain true to traditional English garden bench design, we've kept metal fasteners to a minimum, and used brass, rather than steel, where fasteners can't be avoided.

The legs, arms and back rails are made from 8/4 stock or two pieces of 3/4-in. stock face-glued to create 1 1/2-in.-thick parts. The thickness is needed to support the framework of this hefty bench. The heart of the bench is in the joinery.

Traditional white and yellow wood glues don't withstand moisture well, so all glued joints in this project are made with exterior-grade wood glue, which can be purchased at most building centers or hardware stores.

Finishing

When built with any of the woods discussed above, outdoor furniture will survive many years. But even well-made outdoor furniture should be treated in some fashion both to keep it looking good and to keep the weather from wearing out the wood. The grain of weather-

About white oak

White oak is among the most versatile and beautiful of woods. Both solid white oak and white oak veneers are prized for the attractive flaked, striped figures of quarter-sawn stock. The wood is strong and hard, making it long lasting. It can be used indoors and outdoors—the appearance in the wood pores of a chemical called tyloses makes white oak resistant to moisture.

Grain: The grain is fairly straight and tight—much tighter than red oak.

Color: White oak is a light brown with hints of yellow and occasional streaks of darker browns.

Workability: The straight grain makes white oak fairly easy to work with, although white oak is hard and dull power saw blades will burn the wood. Because of its hardness, white oak should be pre-bored for nailing.

Finishing: Accepts stains evenly. Clear finishes enhance the grain.

Unfinished

With clear topcoat

White oak

worn outdoor furniture can become porous, inviting fungus, mildew and insects.

Applying a clear water repellent with ultraviolet inhibitors is your best protection against weathering. Or you can use spar varnish, a favorite of boat builders. You can choose a repellent with a pigment if you'd like to add some color to the wood. Be sure to add a minimum of two to three coats of repellent or spar varnish to the bottom of the legs, where end grain is liable to soak up moisture.

Maintenance

For the furniture to endure, re-coat it with a preservative every two or three years, depending upon the severity of the climate. Gently scrub the surfaces with a mild detergent and let the surface dry before applying the preservative. Don't forget to wash and coat the leg bottoms.

In harsh climates, store furniture indoors over the winter. If this is not possible, cover the furniture with a heavy plastic sheet. Place spacers, such as wood blocks, between the plastic and the bench to allow air to circulate. If the ground in the storage area is damp, raise the furniture onto wooden blocks.

GARDEN BENCH

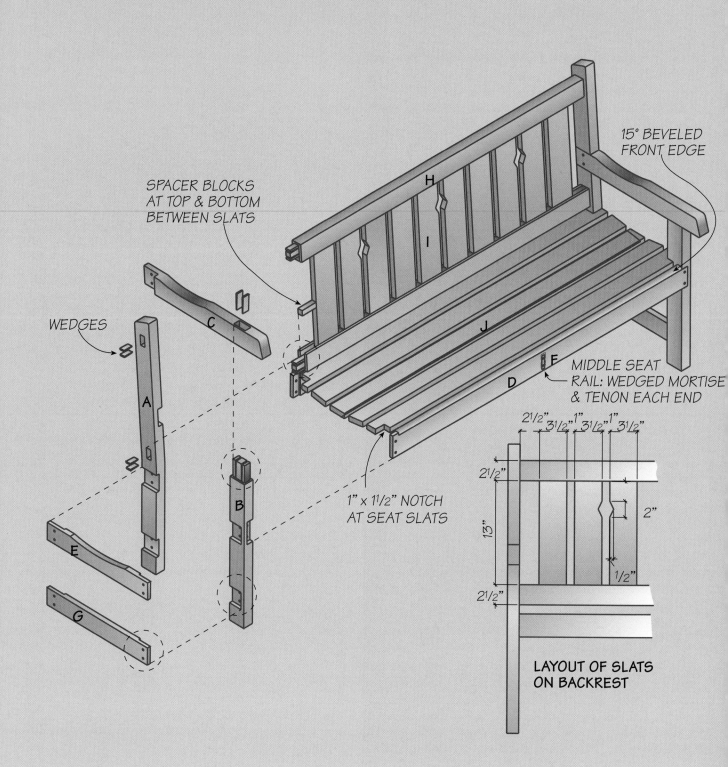

SPACER BLOCKS
AT TOP & BOTTOM
BETWEEN SLATS

15° BEVELED
FRONT EDGE

WEDGES

MIDDLE SEAT
RAIL: WEDGED MORTISE
& TENON EACH END

1" x 1 1/2" NOTCH
AT SEAT SLATS

H

I

J

F

D

A

C

B

E

G

2 1/2"   3 1/2" 1" 3 1/2" 1" 3 1/2"

2 1/2"

13"

2 1/2"

2"

1/2"

LAYOUT OF SLATS
ON BACKREST

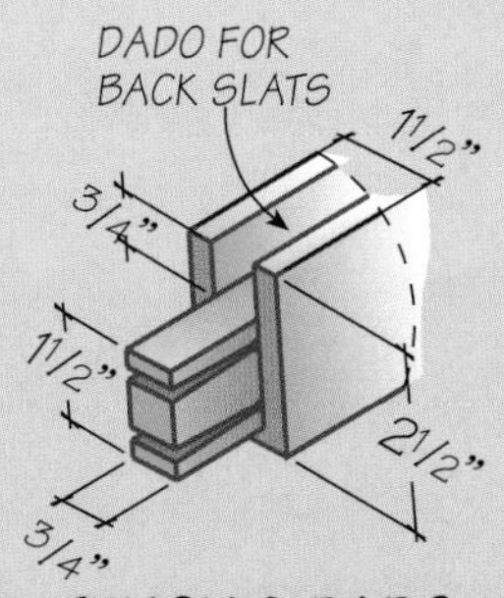
DADO FOR
BACK SLATS
1 1/2"
3/4"
1 1/2"
2 1/2"
3/4"

TENON & DADO
AT BACK RAILS

Garden Bench Cutting List

Part	No.	Size	Material
A. Rear Legs	2	1 1/2 × 2 1/2 × 36″	White Oak
B. Front Legs	2	1 1/2 × 2 1/2 × 23 1/2″	"
C. Arms	2	1 1/2 × 2 1/2 × 21 3/4″	"
D. Front/ Back Seat Rails	2	3/4 × 3 1/4 × 51″	"
E. Side Seat Rails	2	3/4 × 2 1/2 × 17 1/2″	"
F. Middle Seat Rail	1	3/4 × 2 1/2 × 18″	"
G. Lower Side Rails	2	3/4 × 2 1/2 × 17 1/2″	"
H. Back Rails	2	1 1/2 × 2 1/2 × 52″	"
I. Back Slats	10	3/4 × 3 1/2 × 14 1/2″	"
J. Seat Slats	6	3/4 × 2 1/2 × 52″	"

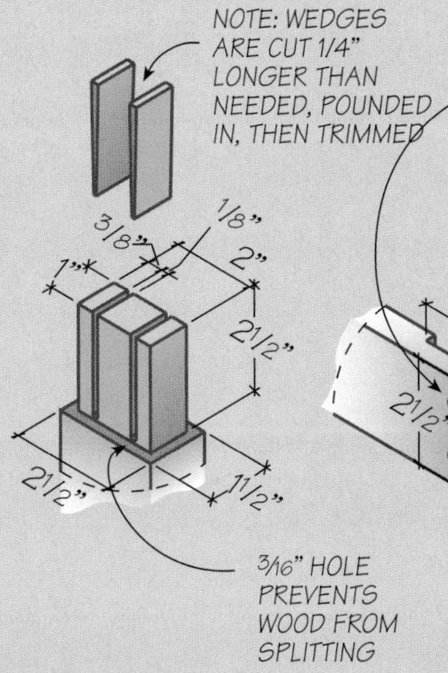
NOTE: WEDGES
ARE CUT 1/4"
LONGER THAN
NEEDED, POUNDED
IN, THEN TRIMMED
3/8"
1/8"
1"
2"
2 1/2"
2 1/2"
1 1/2"
3/16" HOLE
PREVENTS
WOOD FROM
SPLITTING

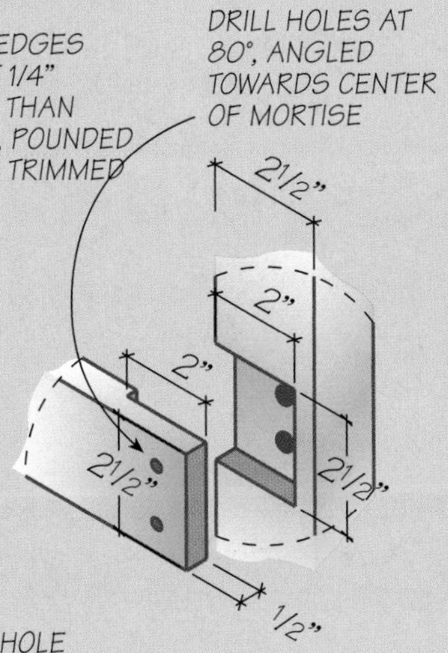
DRILL HOLES AT
80°, ANGLED
TOWARDS CENTER
OF MORTISE
2 1/2"
2"
2"
2 1/2"
2 1/2"
1/2"

WEDGES & TENON AT
TOP OF FRONT LEG

DOWELED BLIND
HALF LAP JOINT

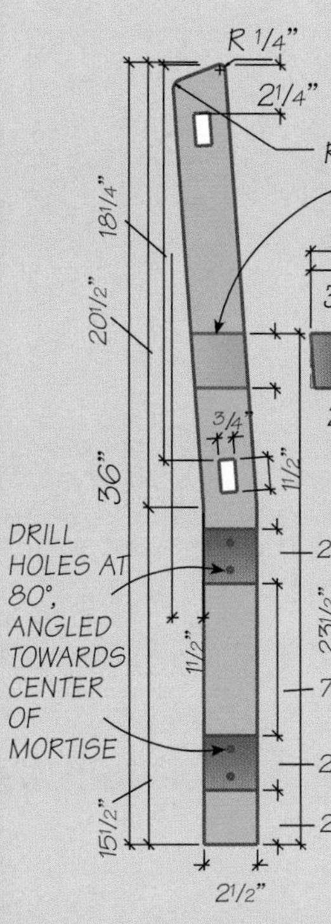
R 1/4"
2 1/4"
R 1/2"
MORTISE IS ON INSIDE OF LEG
18 1/4"
20 1/2"
36"
3/4"
1 1/2"
2 1/2"
1 1/2"
23 1/2"
7"
2 1/2"
2 1/2"
15 1/2"
2 1/2"
DRILL
HOLES AT
80°,
ANGLED
TOWARDS
CENTER
OF
MORTISE

REAR LEG

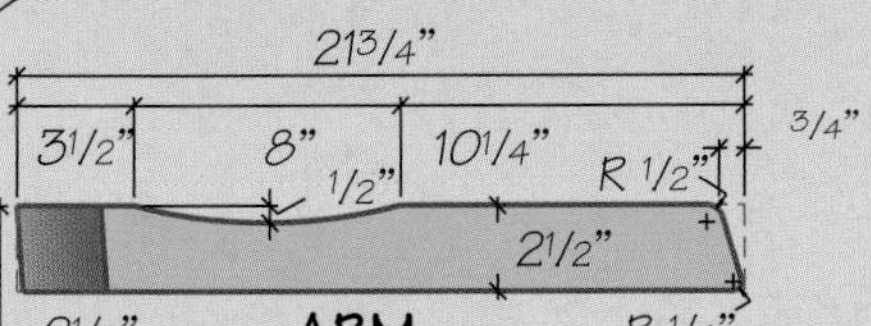
21 3/4"
3 1/2"
8"
10 1/4"
3/4"
1/2"
R 1/2"
2 1/2"
2 1/2"
R 1/4"

ARM

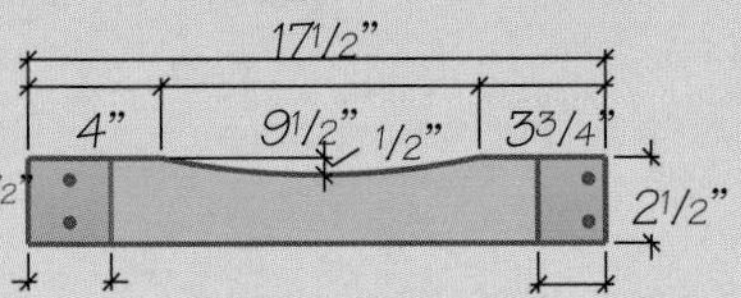
17 1/2"
4"
9 1/2"
1/2"
3 3/4"
2 1/2"
2 1/2"
2"

SIDE SEAT RAIL

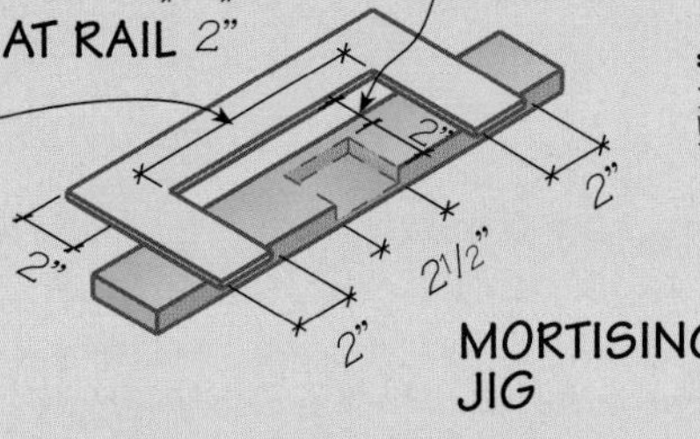
DIST. FROM ROUTER
BASE EDGE TO
CUTTER EDGE
WIDTH OF
MORTISE,
PLUS DIST.
FROM
ROUTER
BASE EDGE
TO CUTTER
EDGE
2"
2"
2"
2 1/2"
2"

MORTISING
JIG

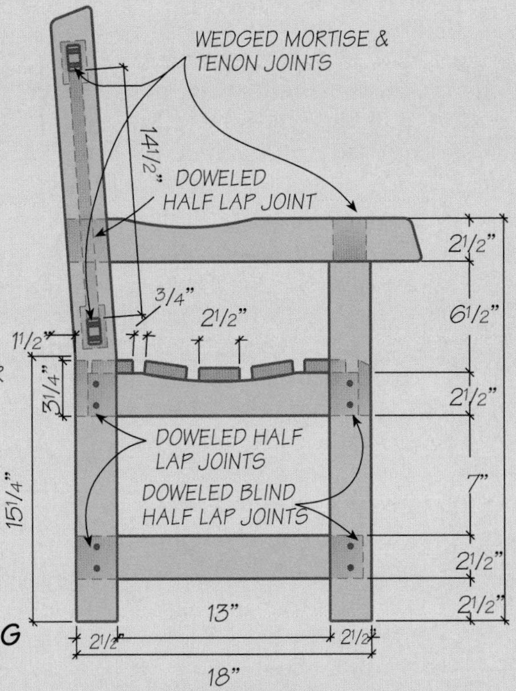
WEDGED MORTISE &
TENON JOINTS
14 1/2"
DOWELED
HALF LAP JOINT
2 1/2"
3/4"
2 1/2"
6 1/2"
1 1/2"
3 1/4"
2 1/2"
DOWELED HALF
LAP JOINTS
DOWELED BLIND
HALF LAP JOINTS
15 1/4"
7"
23 1/2"
2 1/2"
2 1/2"
13"
2 1/2
2 1/2
18"

SIDE VIEW

Project Assembly Steps: Garden Bench

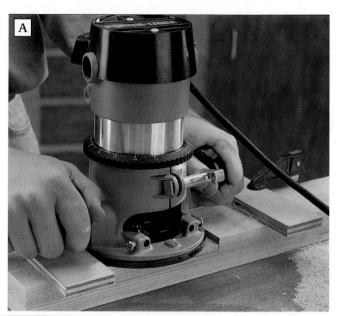

FIGURE A: Cut the leg lap dadoes with a router and straight bit. A simple U-shaped plywood jig makes this task easy because it limits the path of the router and outlines the dado joint (See page 130).

Prepare leg, arm & rail blanks

1 Prepare blanks for the front and rear legs, arms, and top and bottom back rails. Since all of these parts will be 1½ in. thick, you can use 8/4 (2 in.) lumber and plane it down to size, or face-glue two pieces of planed ¾-in.-thick stock (See *Face-gluing,* page 46). Be sure to use an exterior-grade glue, like polyurethane-based glue, for all of the garden bench joinery.

2 Rip-cut and cross-cut the rear leg blanks, arms, and top and bottom back rails to size (See *Cutting list,* page 119).

Cut the rear leg lap dadoes

1 Build two plywood U-shaped half-lap router jigs (See *Doweled half-lap joints,* page 130 and **FIGURE A**). One jig should cut 2½-in.-wide lap dadoes and the other should cut 3¼-in.-wide lap dadoes.

2 Mark with a square and pencil the 2½-in.-wide × ¾-in.-deep dado that will accept the arm lap on each rear leg. The top edge of the dado groove should be 23½ in. from the bottom of the leg. (NOTE: Mark and cut these arm dadoes now, while the legs are straight. This way the arms will remain parallel to the side and lower rails and perpendicular to the front legs even after the top portions of the rear legs are cut at an angle.)

3 Clamp the 2½-in. router jig to each leg and rout the arm lap dado. Remember this is a through-notch, so the dado is cut across the entire face of each leg. Mark these notches as "arm lap" with a pencil.

4 Mark with pencil and square and cut the ½-in.-deep side seat rail through-dadoes in the legs on the faces opposite the arm lap mortises using the 2½-in. router jig. The top edges of these dadoes should be 14½ in. from the bottom of the legs.

FIGURE B: Cut the slope in the rear legs with a jig saw after routing all the leg lap dadoes. This way, you'll avoid machining at an angle, and at the same time keep the arm joints parallel to the rest of the horizontal side members.

5 Lay out and cut ½-in.-deep through-dadoes for the lower rails with the same 2½-in. router jig. The top edge of these dadoes should be 5 in. from the bottom of each leg.

6 Mark with pencil and square the 3¼-in. part-blind lap dado in the back edge of each rear leg to accept the back seat rail. Lay out this cut so the router will enter the back edge of the rear leg on the arm lap side of each leg. Also, position this groove on the leg so that the bottom edge of the bottom back rail will align with the bottom edge of each side seat rail. Since this dado is part-blind, it should be cut across the back edge of the leg, stopping ½ in. from the opposite face of the leg (which also is the bottom of the side seat rail dado groove). This way, the back seat rail will partially align with and butt up against the side seat rail and be covered when you assemble the bench.

7 Clamp the 3¼-in. U-shaped router jig to the back edge of each rear leg and cut these part-blind back seat rail dadoes. Then square the blind corners of the dado with a sharp chisel.

Cut the rear leg angles

1 Lay out the slope for the angle in the upper back portion of each rear leg by first penciling a mark on the front edge of each rear leg blank 15½ in. from the bottom of the leg. Lay both leg blanks on your workbench so the seat and lower rail dadoes on each leg face up. Then butt a combination square against the front of each leg at the 15½ in. mark and pencil a second layout mark across the face, 2½ in. from the front edge. Using a long straightedge, extend a line from this second mark up to the top back corner of each leg blank. Complete each rear leg's back profile by extending the pencil line down to the bottom of each leg, keeping it parallel to the front edge.

2 Clamp each leg securely to the workbench and cut along the back profile layout line with a jig saw **(See FIGURE B)**. It's easiest to do this in two passes by first removing the angled portion of the waste and then removing the rest from the bottom of the leg to the starting point of the angle. Or, you can rip the lower portion of the leg on a band saw with a fence clamped to the saw table. Cut from the bottom of the leg, with the front edge of the leg against the fence and stop cutting when you reach the leg angle.

3 Lay a square against each leg's back angle and scribe two or three reference marks perpendic-

ular to the back angle, 2½ in. from it along its length. Complete the front profile of the leg angle by connecting these marks, using a straightedge, from the top of the leg blank to the 15¼ in. mark on the front of the leg. Cut the remaining waste from the top front of each leg. Your result should be two legs that are 2½ in. wide from top to bottom and slope back gradually above 15½ in. Smooth the edges of both legs with a belt or pad sander and 120-grit sandpaper.

4 Cut the top bevels of each leg by first measuring 1 in. down from the top back corner of each leg. Then draw a line from this point to the top front corner, and cut off the waste with a jig saw or band saw.

Cut the front leg dadoes

1 Butt the edge of a front leg blank to the front edge of each rear leg and align the leg bottoms. Extend side and lower rail dado edge lines from the rear legs across the face of each front leg using a square and pencil. Matching front and rear leg dadoes like this will keep the rails parallel to one another, front to back, when we assemble the bench. Also, mark each front leg as "right" or "left" to keep their orientation straight when you machine the dado grooves. It's easy to get confused when cutting so many joints and cut a joint the wrong direction.

FIGURE C: Dry-assemble all of the members of each side frame, lay each arm blank into position and mark the angle of the through half-lap that joins the arm to the rear leg. Trim off this waste.

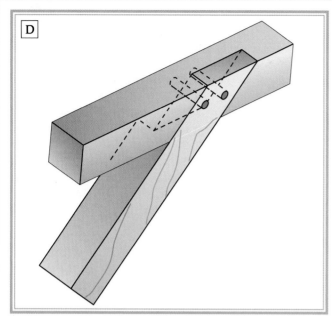

FIGURE D: An angled half-lap joint (pinned).

2 Cut ½-in.-deep part-blind dadoes for the lower rails and side seat rails in each front leg using the 2½-in. router jig. These dadoes should stop ½ in. from the front edge of each front leg. Square the corners with a sharp chisel.

3 Use the lower edge of the side seat rail dado as a reference, and pencil a line across the front edge of each front leg with a square. These refer-

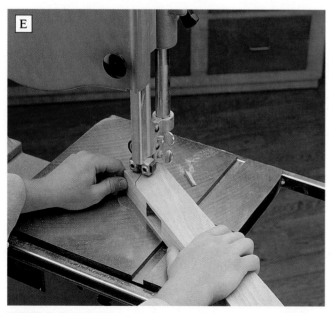

FIGURE E: Slope the front of each arm on the bandsaw after cutting the front leg through-mortise, then smooth out the cut with a smoothing file or sander.

ence lines will mark the lower edge of the part-blind front seat rail dado in each leg. Clamp the 3¼-in. router jig to the front edge of each front leg and orient it so the dado stops ½ in. from the outside face of each leg. Set the router depth to ½ in. and cut the front seat rail dadoes in each front leg.

Cut the tongues in the rails

1 Rip-cut and cross-cut the lower rails, and front, back, side and middle seat rails to size (See *Cutting List,* page 119). All are cut from ¾-in.-thick stock. (NOTE: This would be a good time to bevel the top front edge of the front seat rail on a table saw. The actual angle is not critical—about 15°. Easing this edge will keep the front seat rail from irritating the backs of sitters' knees.)

2 Cut the through-tongues in the side seat rails and lower rails that will fit in the rear leg dadoes. The tongues for these through lap joints are all the same dimension, so you can create one set-up on the table saw and cut them one after another. Use a tenoning jig (See *Tenoning jig,* page 50) and start by cutting the 2½ in.-tall cheeks on the table saw with the fence ½ in. from the blade.

3 Clamp a relief scrap block to the saw fence on the infeed side of the blade and set the fence so that each rail's through tongue, when butted on end against the block, will pass over the blade at 2½ in. and cut each shoulder. (The relief block prevents waste cutoffs from becoming trapped between the blade and fence and flying back at you.) Raise the blade ¼ in. above the saw table, hold each rail with a long edge against the miter gauge, and cut the through tongue shoulders.

4 Reset the saw to cut the blind tongues in the side seat and lower rails that fit into the front legs. Use the same procedure described in steps 1 to 3 to cut the tongues, but cut these tongues so they have have 2-in. cheeks and ¼-in. shoulders.

5 Cut part-blind laps in the front and rear seat rails using the same tenoning sequence. Reset the saw to cut 1-in. cheeks and ¼-in. shoulders.

Cut the angled half-lap arm joints

1 Dry-assemble each side frame (side seat and lower rails, front and rear legs) with clamps and label the parts as "right" or "left". Lay the frames on the workbench, arm lap dado facing up, then lay each arm in position **(See FIGURE C)**.

2 Check the fit of the parts. When the arm blank lays in the rear leg dado, the lower edge of the arm should extend slightly beyond the back edge of the rear leg (because of the leg angle), and the top edges of the arm and the front leg should sit flush.

3 Scribe a line onto each arm, following the angle where it extends beyond the rear leg dado. Also pencil two marks on the outside face of each arm where it intersects with the front and back edge of the front leg. Label each arm as "right" or "left", then disassemble.

4 Lay a sliding T-bevel gauge against an arm and lock it in place at the angle you just transferred from the rear leg. Use the bevel square to set the table saw miter gauge, and cut the angled back edge off of each arm.

5 Build a tenoning jig with a vertical member angled back to match the angle of the bevel square in step 4 (See *Angled half-lap joints*, page 128). Clamp a bench arm in the tenoning jig so the angled end of the arm sits flat on the saw table and a long edge is snug against the vertical member of the jig. Raise the blade to 2½ in., set the fence ¾ in. from the blade, and cut angled cheeks into the backs of both arms.

6 Cut the angled arm lap shoulders by running the arms over the saw blade raised to ¾ in (**See FIGURE D**). Use the miter gauge set to the bevel angle from step 4 when you make the shoulder cuts. Clamp a relief block to the infeed side of the saw fence.

Cut the arm through mortises

1 Lay out the through mortises in the arms for the front leg tenons using the leg/arm intersection marks you drew on the arms as guides. Extend these lines with a square and pencil across the top edge of each arm. The front leg through tenons measure 1 in. wide × 2 in. long, which leaves a ¼-in. shoulder around all four sides. Mark this mortise area between the leg guidelines on top of each arm. Draw a line down the center of each mortise.

2 Drill out the mortise area with a 1-in.-dia. Forstner or spade bit chucked in a drill press.

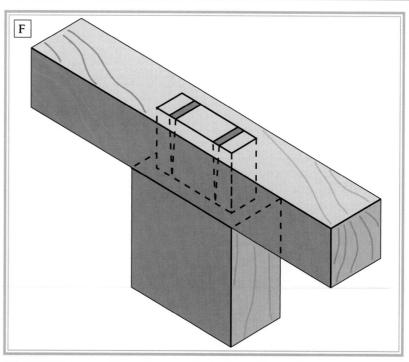

FIGURE F: Wedged mortise-and-tenon joints, used in arm/leg joints.

Center the bit's point on the line you drew that bisects the mortise. Remove the waste in successive passes along the centerline.

3 Scribe the outline of each mortise on the top and bottom of the arm with a chisel or sharp utility knife. Begin to clean up the walls of each mortise, working a sharp chisel from the top and bottom of the arm in toward the center, cutting across the grain. Work with the grain next, until each mortise is square and clean.

4 Cut the front bevels of each arm by first measuring ¾ in. back from the top front corner of each arm. Draw a line from this point to the bottom front corner. Scribe a ½-in. radius to ease the top corner and a ¼-in. radius for the bottom corner. Cut off the waste on the band saw (**See FIGURE E**) or with a jig saw.

Cut the back leg through mortises

1 Use the technical drawings on page 119 as a guide for measuring and laying out two through mortises in the rear legs for the top and bottom back rail tenons. (NOTE: Although these mortises are cut on the angled portion of each leg, they are square with the angle of the leg.) These mortise dimensions are ¾ in. wide × 1½ in. long.

2 Remove the waste as you did for the arm mortises, but using a ¾-in. bit. Clean up the four mortises by first scribing the outline and then chiseling in from each end of the mortise until they are square and clean.

Cut the middle seat rail through mortises

1 Measure and lay out with pencil and square a ½-in.-wide × 2-in.-long mortise in the outside face of the front and back seat rails. Center it left to right on each rail, and position it ¼ in. up from the bottom edge.

2 Mark the centerline of each mortise and drill out the waste with a ½-in. bit in the drill press. Clean and square the mortises with a chisel.

Cut the front leg through tenons

1 Use the tenoning jig/relief block set-up on the table saw to cut cheek and shoulder cuts for the front leg through tenons, checking the set-up first on a test piece. These tenons have 2½-in. cheeks and ¼-in. shoulders. Check the fit of each leg tenon in its arm mortise. Shave the cheeks of the tenons until they fit snugly in the mortises without binding and sit flush with the top edge of each arm.

2 Mark ⅛-in. saw kerf lines across the width of the tenons for the tenon wedges (See **FIGURE F**). Then bore a 3/16-in.-dia. relief hole at the base of each tenon saw kerf. These holes will reduce the

possibility of splitting the three sections of each tenon when you tap home the wedges.

3 Clamp one of the front legs in the tenon jig (tenon end on the table) with its edge against the saw fence and face against the jig's vertical support. Then set the fence ⅝ in. from the blade, raise the blade 2½ in., and cut across the width of the tenon. Flip the leg on edge, reclamp it in the jig, and make the second tenon wedge kerf. Repeat the kerf cuts in the other front leg tenon.

Cut the back rail through tenons

1 Use the tenoning jig/relief block set-up on the table saw to cut tenons with 1½-in. cheeks and ⅜-in. shoulders on the face sides only of the top and bottom back rails. These tenons are offset—top to bottom—on the rails to allow for a dado groove, so don't make the short cheek or shoulder cuts yet.

2 Reset the tenoning jig/relief block set-up to cut 1½-in. cheeks and ¼-in. shoulders in the top edge of the top back rail tenon and the bottom edge of the bottom back rail tenon.

3 Reset the tenoning jig/relief block set-up to cut 1½-in. cheeks and ¾-in. shoulders in the bottom edge of the top back rail tenon and the top edge of the bottom back rail tenon.

4 Check the fit of each back rail tenon in its back leg mortise. Shave the cheeks of the tenons until they fit snugly in the mortises without binding and sit flush with the outside face of each back leg.

5 Mark cutting lines to cut two 1½-in. deep saw kerfs across the width of each back rail tenon, as for the front leg mortises. Drill 3/16-in. relief holes along the base of each kerf. Cut the kerfs on a table saw.

FIGURE G: Dry-fit the top and bottom back rail through tenons into the rear leg mortises so that the rail dadoes face one another. Measure the distance between the rails and add the length of the dadoes to this distance to determine the length of the backrest slats. The slats will be held captive in these dado grooves without glue.

Cut middle seat rail through tenons

1 Clamp the middle seat rail on-end in the tenoning jig with the face of the rail against the fence and set the fence ⅝ in. from the blade. Raise the blade to ¾ in. above the table and pass the rail through the blade. Flip the rail to the other face, clamp it in the jig, and shave the other ¾-in. tenon cheek. Repeat these cuts on the other end of the rail.

Since the face shoulders on this rail are only ⅛ in., cutting these cheeks also cuts the shoulders.

2 Reclamp the rail so a short edge butts against the fence and reset the fence ¼ in. from the blade. Make the ¾-in. cheek cut, flip the workpiece on edge, and complete the other short cheek cut. Then flip the rail end-for-end and duplicate these short cheek cuts on the opposite tenon.

3 Lower the blade to ¼ in. and cut the shoulders on the short ends of both tenons with the workpiece held against the miter gauge. The result should be tenons that measure ½ in. wide × 2 in. long. Test-fit them in the front and back rail mortises and trim them until they fit flush to the face of each rail.

4 Mark cutting lines for two ¾-in.-deep saw kerfs across the width of each middle seat rail tenon. Drill ³⁄₁₆-in. relief holes along the base of each kerf. Cut the wedge kerfs on the table saw.

Cut the back slats

1 Rout a ¾-in.-wide × ¾-in.-deep groove along the top edge of the bottom back rail and in the bottom edge of the top back rail, using a dado-blade set in the table saw. These grooves extend the full length of each rail.

2 Dry-assemble the top and bottom back rails to the rear legs and measure the length of the back slats (See FIGURE G). Be sure to include the additional 1½ in. for the dado grooves.

3 Cut the 10 back slats to size. Line up three sets of two slats and mark a 1-in.-wide × 2-in.-long diamond pattern across the mating edges of each set, 3 in. down from the top (See Diagram, page 118). Make the diamond-shaped cut-outs with a jig saw or band saw.

4 Cut the short filler strips to use as spacers for the back slats. Each strip should be ¾ in. wide × ¾ in. tall. Cut four strips that are 2½ in. long and 18 strips that are 1 in. long.

5 Fit the back slats and filler strips in the bottom rail groove, mark the slat locations with a pencil, then bore a ⅛-in.-dia. weep hole centered on each slat through the groove and out the bottom of the rail (See FIGURE H). Weep holes prevent water from pooling in the groove.

FIGURE H: Drill ⅛-in.-dia. weep holes beneath each back slat and through the bottom back rail. This drainage measure will keep water from collecting in the dado groove, where it can soak into the end grain of the back slats and cause rot.

Cut the arm and seat contours

1 Use the measurements in the drawings on page 119 as a reference to create patterns for making the curved contours in the tops of the arms and side and middle seat rails (See Transfer patterns, page 134). Transfer the pattern outlines to each workpiece and make the contour cuts with a jig saw or band saw. Then smooth the curves with 120-grit sandpaper.

FIGURE I: Glue-up the side frames and clamp the lap joints with C-clamps and wood cauls. Pipe clamps also help to keep the lap joints from sliding out of position.

FIGURE J: Glue the top and bottom back rails into one side frame, slide the back slats into place and glue the rails into the other side. Keep several pipe clamps handy to hold the assembly together.

Machine the wedges

1 Cut oak wedges for all through tenons in the bench. (NOTE: Orient your wedge stock to cut wedge blanks with the grain. Cross-grain wedges will break when you tap them home.) Although the width and length of the wedges will vary with each joint, start by cutting 3/16-in.-thick wedge blanks on the band saw using a fence (See *Wedged tenons,* page 132). Cut each wedge 1/2 in. longer than the depth of the tenon kerf, then trim the extra flush with the surface of the tenon.

2 Form the bevel of each wedge by paring it with a chisel or sanding it to shape on a stationary sander. Make a few more wedges of each size than you'll need in case you break one during assembly.

Glue-up the side frames

1 Glue and clamp together the members of each side frame—front and rear legs, lower and side seat rails and arms—working from the bottom up **(See FIGURE I)**.

2 Glue and insert wedges into the front leg through tenons. Tap the wedges home with a mallet, keeping the amount of penetration equal between wedges. Let the assemblies dry, then trim the wedges flush with a hand saw.

3 Bore two 1-in.-deep, 1/4-in.-dia. dowel holes at an 80° angle into each of the lap joints, spacing

FIGURE K: Glue and clamp the middle and front seat rails into position and square the seat by clamping across both its length and width. Then drive glued wedges into the kerfs of the middle rail tenon and let the bench dry thoroughly. Remove the clamps and pin each lap joint with two dowels pitched at 80° toward the center of each joint. Saw the wedges and dowels flush with the surface of each joint.

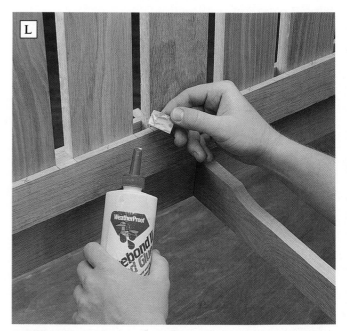

FIGURE L: Glue the back slat filler blocks into position with waterproof glue. They will hold the slats in position, so no further mechanical fasteners are required.

them 1-in. apart vertically and centering them on each tongue (See *Doweled half-lap joints*, page 130). Apply glue and insert 1-in.-long, ¼-in.-dia. dowels, then tap them home. Cut the dowels flush.

Join the sides

1 Dry-fit the top and bottom back rails into the mortises of a side frame and slide the back slats into the rail grooves. Fit the rail tenons into the other side frame. Set the back seat rail into position, insert the middle seat rail tenon into the back rail, and set the front seat rail into place. Check the fit of all the joints and trim or adjust as necessary until the joints fit snugly. We'll follow the same procedure when gluing-up the bench.

2 With the side frame laying on its back, glue the tenons for the top and bottom back rail into a side frame. Place the back slats between the back rails and in the grooves (no glue is needed), and glue the opposite back rail tenons into the other

FIGURE M: Install the seat slats with brass flathead screws and cup washers. Insert wood spacers between the slats at each end of the seat to keep the slats spaced equally. Make sure the counterbored pilot holes for the screws are deep enough that the screw heads are recessed below the surface of the wood.

side frame **(See FIGURE J)**. Clamp the assembly.

3 Insert the wedges into the back rail tenons with glue, tap them home, and let the assembly dry. Cut the wedges flush.

4 Stand the assembly up and glue the middle seat rail tenon into the back seat rail **(See FIGURE K)**. Spread glue into the blind lap dadoes for the front and rear seat rails and the middle seat rail tenon, then clamp these members into place on the bench frame. Apply glue and drive the wedges into the middle seat rail tenons. Let the glue dry.

5 Cut the middle seat rail wedges flush, then drill and install ¼-in.-dia. angled dowels into the front and back seat rail lap joints in the the same fashion as was done when gluing-up the side frames. Cut the dowels flush when the glue dries.

6 Install filler blocks between the back slats in the top and bottom rail grooves with glue **(See FIGURE L)**. Clamp the blocks in place with C-clamps.

Install the seat slats

1 Cut the ¾-in.-thick seat slats to size and space them evenly front to back on the three seat rails. Use spacers to keep the gaps between the slats even. (NOTE: You'll need to notch the front and back seat slats to fit around the front and back legs).

2 Install the seat slats with 1½-in. × #10 flathead brass screws with brass cup washers **(See FIGURE M)**. Drive one screw at each joint between each slat and the side and middle seat rails. Drill counterbored pilot holes for the screws, and make sure the tops of the screw heads are below the surface of the wood in all cases.

Finishing touches

Sand the bench with 120-grit paper, then with 180-grit paper. Apply at least two coats of clear wood protectant or spar varnish (See page 116).

ANGLED HALF-LAP JOINT

Here's an example of an angled half-lap joint reinforced with two dowels that are pinned through the tongue and dado notch. Both ends of the dowels are exposed.

WOODWORKING SKILLS
Making angled half-lap joints

Sooner or later you'll encounter a half-lap situation where the two members of the joint aren't perpendicular to one another. Angled half-laps are common, especially in outdoor furniture where arms join angled back rests of chairs and benches, or when the legs of a table or chair must be braced.

Although the angled and interlocking tongue-and-groove look complicated, tight-fitting angled half lap joints aren't difficult to build. In fact, if you use the following procedure, you won't even have to know the exact angle of the joint. All you need to build angled half-laps is a sliding T-bevel gauge and a modified version of the two-piece tenoning jig you've seen used throughout this book to cut tenons (See page 50).

Cut the dadoed notch in one joint member before you attempt to cut the angled tongue. The assembly sequence shown here begins at this point. NOTE: Although we show a half-lap where both members of the joint are of equal thickness, this technique would also work in situations where the tongue member of the joint is a different thickness (called a modified angled half-lap).

HOW TO MAKE AN ANGLED HALF-LAP JOINT

1 Lay the workpiece to be cut into the angled dado of the other joint member and scribe the tongue angle with a pencil. This line will mark the end of the through-tongue for the lap joint. Scribe another line on the other side to mark the shoulder of the tongue. The lines should be parallel.

2 Transfer the angle of the cutting lines for the tongues to a sliding T-bevel gauge to use as a reference for setting cutting angles throughout the joint-construction project.

Blade guard removed for clarity

3 Lay the sliding T-bevel against the saw blade and adjust the saw's miter gauge until it matches the T-bevel angle to the blade. Then raise the blade, set the workpiece in the miter gauge, and cut the angle along the first pencil line.

4 Use the T-bevel as a guide to set the angle for making a tenoning jig (See page 50).

5 Set the blade height to cut the length of the tongue (the second, inner pencil line drawn in Step 1). Then clamp the workpiece so it rests snugly against the jig with the tongue-end flat on the table. Cut the cheek.

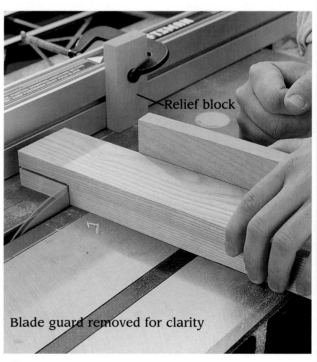

Relief block

Blade guard removed for clarity

6 Reset the blade height to make the shoulder cut, then place the workpiece back in the miter gauge set to the bevel angle. Clamp a relief block to the fence on the infeed side of the blade. Set the fence so the workpiece, when butted against the block, is aligned with the blade. Cut the shoulder. The joint is ready for assembly.

Making doweled half-lap joints

Half-lap joints consist of a wide notch cut into the side of one workpiece to accept a long tongue cut in the other workpiece. In some cases, the tongue extends all the way across the face of the mating piece (a *through half-lap*) and in other cases it stops part way across (a *part blind half-lap*).

When making half-lap joints, cut the notch portion first using a router, a chisel or a table saw equipped with a dado-blade set. We chose to use a router with a straight bit, and a simple U-shaped router guide we made in the shop. The U-shaped guide creates a three-sided straight edge to contain the router base while the material in the notch area is removed.

To make a router guide for cutting a shallow notch, first measure the router setback (the distance from the edge of the router base to the near edge of the bit). Double the setback distance, then add the planned width of the notch. This will give you the required distance between the inside edges of the two arms of the "U". Cut the guide from ½- or ¾-in.-thick plywood, making sure the arms are at least as

long as the setback distance plus the height of the notch. Clamp the guide to your workpiece so the notch is centered between the arms of the guide, and the base of the "U" is square to the notch and positioned so the setback of the router will cut exactly on the base line of the notch.

Make test pieces the same size as the workpieces and test your cuts before making the notch in the actual workpieces. Remove the material in the notch by passing the router bit back and forth across the notch area, following the edges of the guides.

In the sequence below, the notch we cut is *part blind*. For a *through notch*, make sure the bottom of the "U" is set back far enough from the workpiece to allow the router bit to pass all the way across the width and out the other side. When cutting through-notches, you should attach a backer board to the side of the workpiece the router will exit through to keep the wood from tearing out along the edge.

HOW TO MAKE A DOWELED HALF-LAP JOINT

Router setback minus distance from notch to edge of workpiece

2× router setback plus width of notch

1 Outline the notch, then make a U-shaped router guide and clamp it to the workpiece so the guide will contain the router bit within the confines of the notch outline. The notch shown here is part blind (it doesn't extend across the full width of the workpiece), so the bottom of the "U" must be parallel to the bottom of the notch.

2 With a straight bit, rout out the wood in the middle of the notch, freehand. Then, follow along the inside edges of the guide with the router to cut the edges of the notch. Continue cutting until all wood is removed in the notch area and the sides and bottom of the notch are straight and even.

3 Cut the tongue portion of the half-lap joint on your table saw, using a tenoning jig (See page 50). Begin by making the cheek cuts in all workpieces.

Blade guard removed for clarity

4 Cut the shoulders of the tongues on a table saw, using the miter gauge to feed each workpiece past the blade. Clamp a relief block to the fence and measure out from its position to the blade to set up the cut.

5 After gluing and clamping the joint together, bore two dowel holes into the joint at an 80° angle. The dowels should angle toward each other, pinning the joint "dovetail-style" and making it all but impossible for the joint to come apart.

6 Glue dowels into the dowel holes, then cut the ends flush with the surface of the wood using a flexible hand saw.

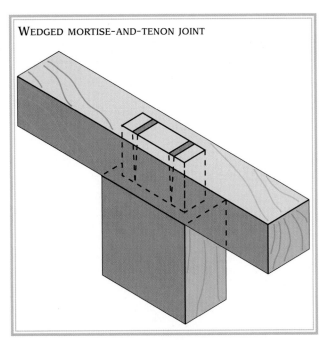

WEDGED MORTISE-AND-TENON JOINT

Hardwood wedges driven into kerf cuts at the ends of a tenon spread the tenon apart, creating a tighter fit in the mortise.

Making wedged-tenon joints

Create strong mortise-and-tenons by cutting mortises all the way through a workpiece and filling them with tenons that come flush to the surface—called a *through* mortise-and-tenon joint. You can strengthen these joints further by driving hardwood wedges into kerf-cuts in the ends of the tenons. As the wedges are driven into each tenon, they spread the tenon so it fits even more snugly in the mortise. In the joint shown here, each tenon is fitted with two wedges. When working with smaller tenons, a single wedge in the middle is probably a better idea.

Wedged mortise-and-tenon joints are very popular for building furniture. In addition to their inherent strength, they also provide an interesting design feature. For even more appeal, you can use wood of contrasting color for the wedges, like walnut wedges in a maple tenon.

HOW TO MAKE A WEDGED MORTISE-AND-TENON JOINT

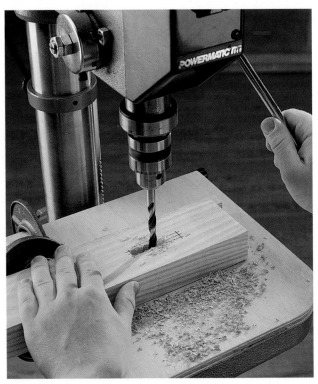

1 Cut the mortise so it goes all the way through the workpiece—insert a backer board between the workpiece and the worksurface first. We used the drill-press method of cutting mortises (page 48), since a standard straight router bit would be too short to make this cut.

2 Cut the tenon (See page 50) and draw a pair of reference lines to divide the tenon into three equal parts. These lines mark the locations of the kerf cuts you'll make to house the wedges. Drill a hole at the point where each line meets the tenon shoulder to help prevent the tenon from breaking when the wedges are driven into it.

3 Make kerf cuts at least ⅛ in. thick into the tenon at the reference lines. We used a tenoning jig (See page 50) to feed the workpiece past the saw blade.

4 Cut 3⁄16-in.-thick wedge blanks that are the same width as the tenon and about ½ in. longer. Use a band saw with a fence to saw the wedge blanks from a piece of stock. Now form the bevels of the wedges by paring them with a chisel or sanding them so they taper from 3⁄16 in. at the top to 1⁄16 in. at the bottom. Make sure the wedges are cut so the wood grain runs lengthwise.

5 Glue and assemble the joint, then apply glue to all sides of one wedge. Drive the wedge partially into one of the tenon kerfs with a wood mallet. Glue and drive the second wedge part-way. Finish driving the wedges by alternating mallet blows between them or driving them both at the same time.

6 When the glue dries, trim the wedges flush with the wood surface using a hand saw with a flexible blade.

HOW TO TRANSFER PATTERNS

1 To transfer patterns to a workpiece, begin by drawing a full-size grid either on hardboard or directly onto your workpiece (cut to size). If the grid drawing in your plans notes that each square equals 1 in., draw 1-in. squares.

WOODWORKING SKILLS
Making and using transfer patterns

Many woodworking project plans come with grid patterns to help you lay out and cut complicated contours. The most direct way to accomplish this is to lay out the contour onto the workpiece itself, using the pattern as a reference.

Grid patterns will indicate the scale of the grid. To make use of the pattern, you'll need to determine the scale: for example, the pattern may indicate that ½ in. equals 1 in., in which case you should plot out a pattern of 1 in. grids on the workpiece. Be very careful that the grid pattern you draw is square and the pattern is oriented correctly on the workpiece.

You can also use this method to create a template from hardboard (See *Templates*, page 29). Woodworkers who enjoy more technologically advanced methods may prefer to use a photocopier to enlarge a grid pattern to full size, then tape it to the workpiece.

2 Note where each line of the scale drawing crosses a grid line, and make a corresponding mark on the full-size squares. Locate key points that do not fall on a line and mark them between the lines on your enlarged grid. When all the marks are made, connect them as smoothly as you can.

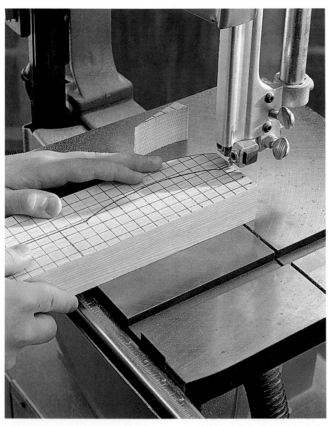

3 Use a band saw, scroll saw or jig saw to make the contour cut. Cut just outside the layout line.

4 Clamp the contoured workpiece in a vise and use a cabinet scraper or smoothing rasp to smooth-out the cut.

5 Sand the contour. An oscillating spindle sander is ideal for this job. Otherwise, you can use a drum sander attachment mounted in your drill press, or simply hand-sand the workpiece.

6 Use the contoured workpiece as a template for tracing the pattern onto additional workpieces.

Cherry Hope Chest

For graduations, weddings, birthdays or just to say you care there is no better gift for a daughter or granddaughter than a beautiful hope chest you made with your own hands. The beauty of cherry and the charm of hand-cut dovetail joints give this hope chest special appeal.

Woodworking Skills You'll Learn:

- **Designing a chest**

- **Attaching a chest lid or table top with sliding-dovetail battens**

- **Working with tongue-and-groove liner panels**

- **Cutting decorative edge profiles with a router**

- **Making finger joints**

- **Cutting sliding dovetails**

- **Making hand-cut dovetail joints**

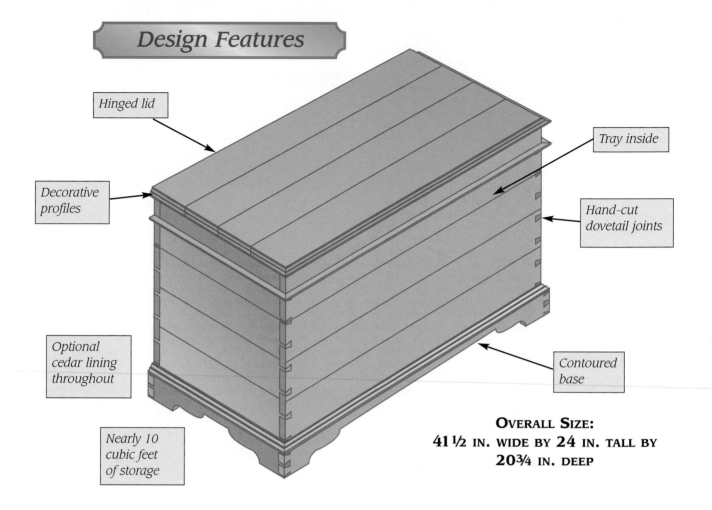

Hinged lid

Decorative profiles

Optional cedar lining throughout

Nearly 10 cubic feet of storage

Tray inside

Hand-cut dovetail joints

Contoured base

OVERALL SIZE:
41 ½ IN. WIDE BY 24 IN. TALL BY
20¾ IN. DEEP

PROJECT NO. 7:

Cherry Hope Chest

Hope chests are among the most endearing gifts you can make for a daughter or a granddaughter. Traditionally, the hope chest is used to store personal heirlooms and keepsakes. The name derives from the common practice of using the hope chest to store a family wedding gown that represents a young woman's hope to meet and marry the man of her dreams. The chest is sized to be set at the foot of the bed, where it has practical use for storing sweaters, blankets and miscellaneous finery.

General planning

When the first immigrants came to America, very often the only furnishing they brought along was the family chest, filled with the most valuable family possessions. At that time, chestbuilding was recognized as a true artform. Most chests were of heirloom quality,

made from the finest hardwood and featuring intricate joinery and amazingly detailed woodcarvings and trim moldings. Today, much of the decorative detailing has passed to the wayside, but the primary issues encountered when planning a chest are essentially the same: the type of wood and joinery to use, and the style and quantity of decorative embellishments.

Parts of a chest. A chest is comprised of three separate parts: a *carcase*, a *base* and a *lid*. The carcase is simply a box with a bottom panel. The carcase rests on the base, which usually has feet of some kind for stability. Chest lids can be a single wood slab or, as in our chest, a small five-sided box consisting of a frame and a top. Some lids rest on or inside the carcase, but most often they're hinged to the back. It's also common to build a compartmentalized tray to fit inside the top of the carcase.

Dimensions. A hope chest is usually a minimum of 20 in. tall, 18 in. deep and 40 in. wide. You can make it up to a few inches larger or smaller in any dimension. Be aware that it doesn't take too much variance from the standard proportions to end up with a chest that has a boxy, clunky feel to it. If you're unsure of the dimensions you've selected, it's a good idea to make a full-scale model of the planned size by taping together pieces of cardboard.

Materials. This hope chest is made of solid cherry, a hardwood renown for its rich orange-red color and traditionally used for chests of all varieties. The tray is made from thinner pieces of cherry stock, except for the lauan plywood tray bottom. We built the bottom of the chest from plywood to minimize the problem of wood expansion and contraction here and to save on materials cost. We've also included information for lining the chest with tongue-and-groove strips of aromatic cedar—an optional detail you may want to consider if you're storing textiles of any type in the chest.

Aesthetics. The dovetail joints used to join the carcase, lid and feet are typical of both hope chests and blanket chests. In addition to being very strong, the hand-cut dovetails are also the key design element of our chest. The exposed end grains and the angles of through dovetail joints are fascinating to examine (and they're also a good forum to display your craftsmanship). Nailed-on moldings and router-profiled edges also contribute to the design, along with the solid brass chest handles.

Construction details

The carcase and lid for this hope chest are built from solid cherry panels that are edge-glued together. The lid is attached to the carcase with a continuous hinge, also known as a piano hinge. The carcase is supported by a cherry base with scrolled feet. A flat frame with mitered corners is mounted to the top of the base to form the base assembly. The assembly is built separately and attached to the carcase with screws driven up through the flat frame.

The tray spans the full dimensions of the carcase opening, actually sitting above the top edge of the carcase. It rests on ¾-in.-thick cleats attached to the inside of the carcase.

Joinery. The sides, front and back of both the carcase and the lid are each built as one panel. This allows you to lay out and cut the dovetail joints first, then

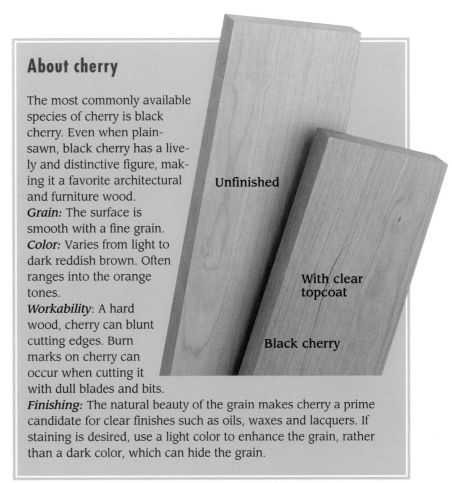

About cherry

The most commonly available species of cherry is black cherry. Even when plain-sawn, black cherry has a lively and distinctive figure, making it a favorite architectural and furniture wood.

Grain: The surface is smooth with a fine grain.

Color: Varies from light to dark reddish brown. Often ranges into the orange tones.

Workability: A hard wood, cherry can blunt cutting edges. Burn marks on cherry can occur when cutting it with dull blades and bits.

Unfinished

With clear topcoat

Black cherry

Finishing: The natural beauty of the grain makes cherry a prime candidate for clear finishes such as oils, waxes and lacquers. If staining is desired, use a light color to enhance the grain, rather than a dark color, which can hide the grain.

CEDAR LINER

To keep the contents of the chest protected from moths and smelling fresh, you can line the chest interior with aromatic cedar closet liner. Closet liner is normally sold in packages containing enough tongue-and-groove strips to cover 15 square feet. Cedar contains natural oils that repel insects. To maintain the aroma, do not apply a finish to the cedar. Sand it lightly to revitalize the aroma when it dissipates.

This antique frame-and-panel chest (left) has a slightly formal appearance that makes it suitable for living rooms, dining rooms and parlors, where it can be used for storing throws, table linens or even outerwear. Cherry, walnut or oak would be good wood choices for this chest.

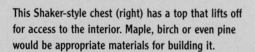

This Shaker-style chest (right) has a top that lifts off for access to the interior. Maple, birch or even pine would be appropriate materials for building it.

Here's a six-board storage chest with decorative grooving that could be cut with a router. The corners can be made using most common types of wood joints. This general type of chest occasionally features an internal framework that provides corner support and creates a ledge for supporting a tray.

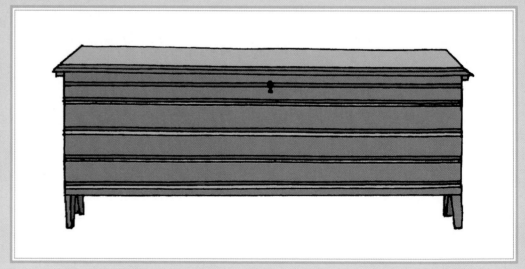

rip-cut the parts of the lid to size from the top of each panel. That way, you're guaranteed that the dovetail joints and wood grain will be well matched and in perfect alignment. The base is also made with hand-cut dovetails (but the joints are made directly on the base parts after they're cut to size).

The top of the lid is a glued-up panel attached to the frame with battens. The battens feature sliding dovetail pins at each end. The pins fit into dovetail tails cut in the top edges of the frame pieces. The method secures the top while still allowing it to move slightly as the wood in the chest expands and contracts.

The compartmentalized tray is made with finger joints cut in a router table using a special cutter. The sides and dividers are made of ½-in. cherry resawn from thicker stock.

Trim. The decorative trim on the lid and the top portion of the base assembly is made by routing a strip of cherry with a piloted double Roman ogee router bit. The routed strip is rip-cut to width, then attached with wire nails.

Hardware. Other than the wire nails used to attach the trim and the cedar liner strips, the only metal fasteners used in this project are the wood screws used to attach the carcase to the base assembly and to attach the top panel to the lid frame. Other hardware needed includes the 1½-in.-wide brass piano hinge, the brass lid supports, and the two brass chest handles for the sides of the chest.

Finishing. Bring out the beautiful cherry color and grain with a natural finish that penetrates the wood pores—oil. The oils typically used to finish furniture include tung oil, boiled linseed oil and Danish oil. The latter is a blend of oil and varnish and provides a satin surface, rather than a glossy one. It's also the easiest of products to apply, and requires only two coats.

You can wipe on Danish oil with a clean, lint-free cloth. Make sure to wipe off any excess, or else it will become tacky as it dries. In addition, look for beading during the day after you've applied the finish. Remove beads with a clean, dry cloth. Allow the finish to cure overnight, then sand with 280-grit paper. Apply a second coat. If you wish, you can smooth the final coat by wet-sanding it with Danish oil and 600-grit paper. Be sure to remove any excess with a clean, dry cloth.

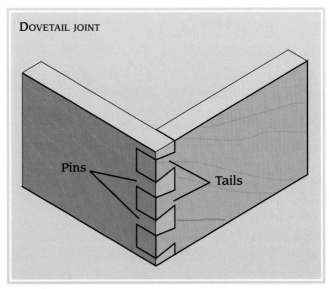

Dovetail joints are used to join the sides, front and back of the chest.

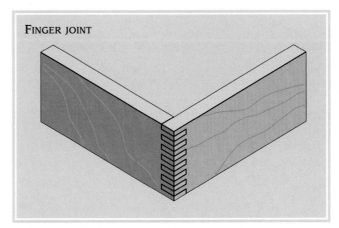

Finger joints are used to assemble the corners of the tray.

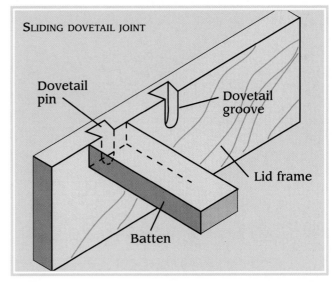

Sliding dovetails are used to join the battens that secure the top of the lid to the sides of the lid frame.

CHERRY HOPE CHEST

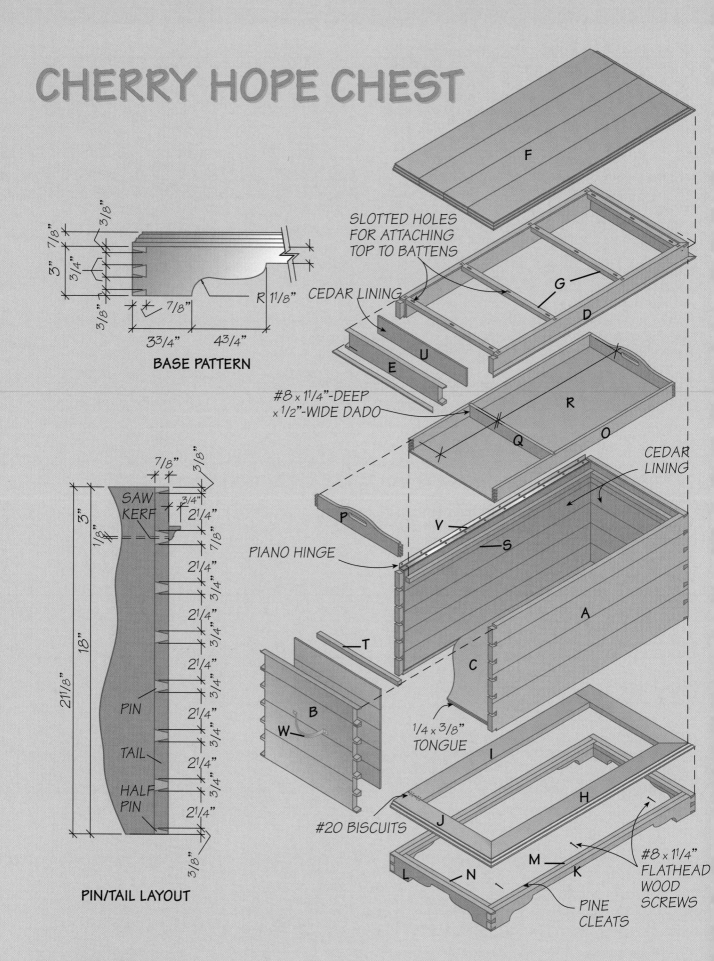

BASE PATTERN

3/8"
7/8"
3"
3/4"
3/8"
3/8"
7/8"
R 1 1/8"
3 3/4"
4 3/4"

PIN/TAIL LAYOUT

7/8"
3/8"
SAW KERF
3"
1/8"
3/4"
2 1/4"
7/8"
18"
2 1/4"
3/4"
2 1/4"
3/4"
21 1/8"
2 1/4"
3/4"
2 1/4"
3/4"
PIN
2 1/4"
3/4"
TAIL
2 1/4"
3/4"
HALF PIN
2 1/4"
3/8"

F

SLOTTED HOLES FOR ATTACHING TOP TO BATTENS

CEDAR LINING

G

D

E

U

#8 x 1 1/4"-DEEP x 1/2"-WIDE DADO

R

Q

O

CEDAR LINING

P

PIANO HINGE

V

S

A

T

C

1/4 x 3/8" TONGUE

I

B

W

H

#20 BISCUITS

J

L

N

M

K

#8 x 1 1/4" FLATHEAD WOOD SCREWS

PINE CLEATS

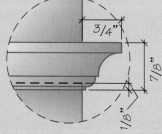

PROFILE @ TOP

7/8"

3/4"

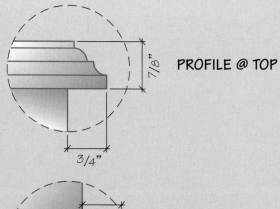

3/4"

7/8"

1/8"

PROFILE @ BOTTOM OF LID

Cherry Hope Chest Cutting List

Part	No.	Size	Material
CARCASE			
A. Front/Back	2	7/8 × 18 × 40"	Cherry
B. Sides	2	7/8 × 18 × 20"	"
C. Bottom	1	3/4 × 19 × 39"	Cherry Plywood
LID ASSEMBLY			
D. Lid Front/Back	2	7/8 × 3 × 40"	Cherry
E. Lid Sides	2	7/8 × 3 × 20"	"
F. Top	1	7/8 × 20 × 41½"	"
G. Battens	4	3/4 × 7/8 × 19¼"	"
BASE ASSEMBLY			
H. Base Frame Front	1	7/8 × 3 × 41½"	"
I. Base Frame Back	1	7/8 × 3 × 35½"	"
J. Base Frame Sides	2	7/8 × 3 × 20¾"	"
K. Base Front/Back	2	7/8 × 3 × 41½"	"
L. Base Sides	2	7/8 × 3 × 20¾"	"
M. Base Cleats	2	3/4 × 3/4 × 39¾"	Pine
N. Base Cleats	2	3/4 × 3/4 × 17½"	
TRAY			
O. Front/Back	2	1/2 × 2¼ × 37"	Cherry
P. Sides	2	1/2 × 3¼ × 17⅝"	"
Q. Partition	1	1/2 × 2 × 17⅛"	"
R. Bottom	1	1/4 × 17⅛ × 36½"	Lauan Plywood
S. Tray Cleats	2	3/4 × 3/4 × 37¾"	Cherry
T. Tray Cleats	2	3/4 × 1 × 17¼"	"
CEDAR LINING			
U. Carcase/Lid Interior	32 sq. ft. × 1/4 × 3⅞"		Tongue-in-groove Cedar*
HARDWARE			
V. Brass Piano Hinge	1	1½" (open) × 38"	
W. Brass Handles	2		

*NOTE: Tongue-in-groove cedar sold in nominal 5/16" thickness. Actual thickness is 1/4".

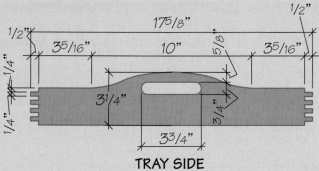

17⅝"

1/2"   1/2"

3⁵/₁₆"   10"   5/8"   3⁵/₁₆"

1/4"

3¼"   3/4"

3¾"

TRAY SIDE

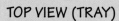

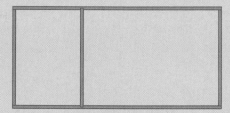

TOP VIEW (TRAY)

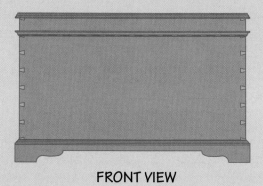

FRONT VIEW

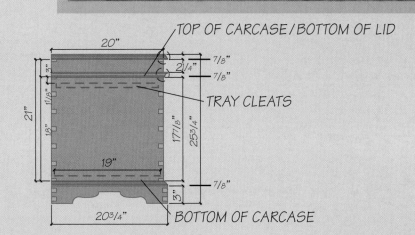

TOP OF CARCASE / BOTTOM OF LID

20"

3"

2¼"

7/8"

7/8"

TRAY CLEATS

11⅛"

21"

18"

17⅛"

25¾"

19"

7/8"

3"

20¾"

BOTTOM OF CARCASE

Project Assembly Steps: Cherry Hope Chest

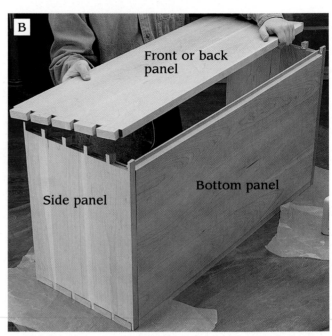

FIGURE B: Assemble and glue the dovetail joints in the carcase one at a time, making the rabbet-and-stopped dado joints between the bottom panel and the carcase panels as you work.

Prepare the glued-up panels

1 Carefully select the boards for the five panels you'll glue-up: the two sides, the front, the back and the lid top. Note that the finished width (height) of the sides, front and back of the chest is 18 in. However, the glued-up panels for these parts should be 21⅛ in. wide because the 3-in.-wide lid sides, front and back are ripped from these panels after the dovetails are cut. The extra ⅛ in. allows for the blade kerf. Edge-glue the boards to create the six panels (See *Edge-gluing,* pages 86 to 88).

2 Rip-cut and cross-cut the panels to finished dimensions (but don't separate the lid parts and carcase parts yet). Remove dried glue and smooth the panels.

Lay out & cut the dovetail joints

1 Lay out the dovetails on the side, front and back panels using the drawing on page 128 as a guide (See *Hand-cut dovetails,* pages 150 to 153). Make sure the middle of the second pin from the

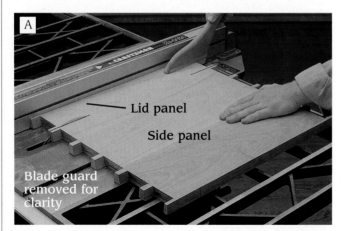

FIGURE A: Rip-cut the lid parts from the glued-up panels after cutting the dovetail joints. To make sure that tear-out from the saw blade doesn't damage the dovetail pin, start the cut on one end, then flip the workpiece and cut from the opposite end until the cuts meet.

top falls exactly 3 in. down from the top of each side panel—you'll rip-cut through this pin when you separate the lid parts and carcase parts.

2 Cut the pins and tails for each joint. We hand-cut the dovetails with a dovetail saw and chisel. If you've got some experience cutting dovetails with a router and dovetailing jig, you can use that method instead.

Cut the lid & carcase parts from the panels

1 Rip-cut the 3-in.-wide lid parts from the tops of the panels containing the carcase front, back and sides, using your table saw. The blade will be ripping the second pin from the top in half. To prevent tearing the pins, make each cut in two passes. After setting the fence to make a 3-in.-wide rip cut, make the first pass just 2 or 3 in. into the panel, then carefully back the piece away from the blade. **CAUTION: Make sure to maintain firm pressure on the workpiece, keeping it snug against the fence as you back it away.**

2 Flip the workpiece and make the second pass, starting at the opposite end of the cutting line **(See FIGURE A).** As the blade nears the kerf from

the first pass, carefully push the panel forward, exerting equal pressure on each end. Use a push stick to feed the 3-in.-wide portion of the panel.

Cut the joints for the bottom panel

The plywood bottom panel attaches to the sides, front and back of the chest carcase with rabbet-and-stopped dado joints. The ¼-in.-thick × ⅜-in.-deep dadoes are cut ½ in. up from the bottom of each carcase panel, and stopped ½ in. from each end. Then, the bottom panel is routed to create a ¼-in.-thick × ⅜-in.-wide rabbet tongue on the tops of all four sides. When the carcase is assembled, the rabbet tongues slip into the stopped dadoes.

1 Install a ¼-in. straight bit in your plunge router and set the cutting depth to cut ⅜ in. deep. Use a straightedge cutting guide to set up for a cut ½ in. up from the bottom of each carcase panel (See *Dadoes & rabbets,* page 26). Start the dado cut ½ in. in from the end of each panel and stop the cut ½ in. from the other end. Cut stopped dadoes in both sides, the front and the back.

2 Cut the bottom panel to size. Then rout a ⅝-in.-thick × ⅜-in.-deep rabbet groove on all four edges of the bottom panel to create a ¼-in.-thick × ⅜-in.-wide rabbet tongue all the way around the top of the board. Remove the material in at least two passes with a straight router bit.

Assemble the carcase

1 Before gluing up the carcase, dry-assemble each joint, one corner at a time. It's not necessary, or even advisable, to dry-assemble the entire chest at once because you can damage the pins during assembly or breakdown.

2 Apply glue to the tops of the pins and the inside faces of the tails. Assemble the carcase with the unglued bottom panel in place (**See FIGURE B**). Use a block of wood (to protect the joints) and a hammer to tap the dovetail joints together. Because well-made dovetails fit together so tightly, you shouldn't need to use clamps.

Make the lid

The top of the chest lid is attached to the lid frame with screws driven through four battens that span between the front and back members of the lid frame. Dovetail-shaped grooves are cut into the top edges of the front and back of the frame. The battens have a sliding dovetail pin cut into each end so they can slide down into the grooves (See

FIGURE C: Glue the dovetailed battens into the dovetail grooves in the inside edges of the of the lid frame, front and back.

FIGURE D: Attach the chest top panel by driving wood screws through slotted holes in the battens and into the underside of the top panel.

Lid battens, page 156).

1 Cut four ⅞-in.-deep dovetail grooves in the top, inside edges of the lid front and back, using a router with a ¾-in. dovetail bit. The first and last groove should be about 2 in. in from the end of each board, and the two inner grooves should be spaced evenly between the outer grooves. It's important that the grooves in the front frame board are aligned with the grooves in the back frame board.

2 Assemble and glue the lid frame. Because there are fewer dovetail joints in the lid frame than in the carcase, you may need to use bar clamps to hold the frame together while the glue sets. Check the diagonals to make sure the frame is square.

3 Make the battens by cutting strips of ⅞-in.-thick cherry to 19¼ in. long (double-check the length by measuring between the bottoms of two dovetail grooves opposite one another in the lid frame), then cutting dovetail profiles in the ends. Mount the dovetail bit in your router table and use a tenoning jig (See page 50) to guide the ends of the battens past the bit. Work on test pieces first to ensure that the dovetail pins fit properly into the grooves.

4 Drill three counterbored guide holes for the wood screws in each batten. Ream the end guide holes slightly to give them a slotted shape. Glue the battens into the dovetail grooves **(See FIGURE C)**.

5 Trim the lid top, if needed, so it fits on top of the lid frame, flush on all sides. To install the top, lay it on a worksurface with the better face down, then lay the lid assembly on the top. Make sure the edges are flush, then extend pilot holes into the top. Drive wood screws through the pilot holes in the battens to attach the top **(See FIGURE D)**. Do not glue these joints.

Build the base assembly

1 The base is comprised of a flat frame laid on top of an upright frame-style pedestal with scrollwork on the bottom edges that creates feet at the corners. Cut the base parts to size.

FIGURE E: After assembling the chest base, install cleats on the inside of the frame, flush with the top edges. The cleats provide a screwing surface for attaching the flat base frame to complete the base assembly.

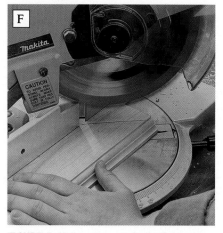

FIGURE F: Make miter cuts in the flat frame members with a miter saw, after cutting decorative profiles.

FIGURE G: Use two biscuits (or dowels, if you prefer) to reinforce the mitered joints in the flat base frame.

2 Lay out and cut dovetail joints in the front, back and sides, according to the dimensions on the drawing on page 128 (See *Hand-cut dovetails*, pages 150 to 153).

3 Make a hardboard template of the base contour shown on page 128 (See *Templates,* page 29). Use the template to lay out cutting lines on all four pieces of the base. Make the contour cuts on a band saw or with a jig saw. Remove saw marks with a smoothing file, then sand.

4 Assemble and glue the dovetail joints to make the base frame; clamp if needed. Cut and install base cleats with glue and screws **(See FIGURE E)**. The flat base frame will be attached to the base by screwing through these cleats.

5 Rip the base frame pieces to width, then rout decorative edges in the front and side base frame pieces with a double Roman ogee bit in a router or router table (See inset photo, *FIGURE M,* page 148).

6 Cut the base frame parts to length. Miter-cut the ends of the front piece and the front ends of the side pieces to 45° **(See FIGURE F)**.

7 Cut two biscuit slots in each base frame joint, then assemble the frame with glue and biscuits. **(See FIGURE G** and *Biscuit joints,* page 106).

8 Attach the base frame to the base cleats from below with #10 × 1½-in. flathead brass wood screws. Countersink the screws.

Attach the base assembly to the carcase

1 The carcase is screwed to the flat frame part of the base assembly. Lay the carcase upside-down on a flat worksurface. Place the base on the carcase and align it. The base and carcase should be flush in back, with equal overhang on the sides and front.

2 Bore screw shank holes through the base frame and pilot holes in the carcase bottom. Install the base with #10 × 1½ in. wood screws **(See FIGURE H)**.

Attach the lid to the carcase

1 Use a continuous (piano) hinge to attach the lid. The hinge is installed in a stopped mortise cut into the mating edges of the lid and the carcase back. Use a router with a straight bit and a cutting guide to cut ¾-in-wide × 38-in.-long mortises for the hinge plates in the bottom of the lid frame and the top of the carcase. The depth of the mortises should equal the thickness of the hinge plates.

2 Lay the hinge in place and mark the screw-hole locations. Drill pilot holes, then attach the hinge to carcase. Rest the lid on the carcase and attach the other hinge plate in the mortise in the lid **(See FIGURE I)**.

FIGURE H: Attach the base assembly to the bottom of the carcase with wood screws driven up through the flat frame portion of the base.

FIGURE I: Join the lid and carcase with a piano hinge set into mortises in the top edge of the back panel and the bottom edge of the lid back.

FIGURE J: Install strips of aromatic cedar to line the chest (optional). The tongue-and-grooved strips are installed much like floorboards, using wire nails.

FIGURE K: Glue and clamp the tray frame members together. Use bar or pipe clamps and small clamping blocks to create even clamping pressure in every direction.

FIGURE L: Glue the partition into the dadoes in the front and back of the tray, then drive a few nails up through the tray and bottom and into the partition for reinforcement.

Install the cedar liners (optional)

1 If you elect to line your hope chest with aromatic cedar (See page 139), install the liner strips to cover the bottom first. Cut the strips to length, then lay them in place. Orient the first piece with the groove against the front, then toe-nail the piece in place with 1 in. brass wire nails. The nail should enter the cedar at the juncture where the tongue meets the shoulder. Use three to five nails in each piece. Continue until the last piece is installed in the bottom. Adjust the width on the last piece by rip-cutting the tongue side of the strip.

2 Install the lining on the front and back next. Start with the grooved edge down to make it easier to nail as you go. (See FIGURE J). Rip the last piece to fit. Line the sides and the lid in the same manner.

Build the tray

1 Resaw (See *Resawing*, pages 70 to 71) or plane cherry stock to ½ in. thickness to make the sides of the tray frame.

2 The frame for the tray is made with finger joints at the corners (See *Finger joints*, page 154). To make accurate finger joints, first rip-cut the sides of the frame to 3¼ in. wide. Don't cut the front and back yet. The method that follows ensures that the front, back and sides will be of equal width (2¼ in.) and that the finger joints will fit together properly.

3 Use a combination square to lay out the straight part of the joint pattern on the sides. Draw the curved portion of the pattern (the handle shapes) using the *Tray Side* drawing on page 143 as a guide.

4 Set your table saw fence or band saw fence to 2¼ in. from the blade. Cut the front and back of the tray frame to width. Make the straight portion of each width cut in the tray sides on the band saw, backing the workpieces out when you reach

Blade guard removed for clarity

FIGURE M: After routing a decorative profile into one edge with a double Roman ogee bit (inset photo), rip-cut the profiled edges of the cherry strips on your table saw to form ¾-in.-wide molding strips.

the curved portion of the pattern. Cut the handle contours in the sides, including the cutout, with a scroll saw or jig saw.

5 Cut a ¼-in. × ¼-in. rabbet for the tray bottom in the inside bottom edge of each tray member. Use a router and ¼ in. straight bit, or make the cuts on your table saw.

6 Set up a box-joint jig on your table saw and cut the joints (See *Finger joints,* page 154). Before assembling the tray, cut the ¼-in.-thick dadoes for the partition in the front and back, using a router and straight bit.

7 Assemble and glue the tray frame. Use bar or pipe clamps with small clamping blocks to apply even pressure in each direction **(See FIGURE K)**. Make sure the frame is exactly square.

8 Cut the tray bottom to fit the rabbeted opening in the bottom of the tray frame, and install it with glue and ⅞-in. brads.

9 Cut the partition to length and glue it into the dadoes in the tray front and back, making sure all the top edges are flush. **(See FIGURE L)**. Drive a few nails through the tray bottom into the bottom edge of the partition.

10 Cut the tray cleats and attach them to the inside of the carcase, 2 in. down from the top edge on all sides, using glue and finishing nails.

Install the moldings
We used decorative moldings to cover the joint where the lid meets the carcase and to frame the top of the lid. Solid cherry moldings large enough for our project are hard to find, so we cut our own.

1 Install a piloted double Roman ogee bit in your router and rout a decorative edge from ¾-in.-wide cherry stock. Shape enough stock to create all your moldings (See *Inset photo,* **FIGURE M**).

2 Rip-cut the shaped boards to width on your table saw to create the moldings (See **FIGURE M**). Miter-cut all the moldings to fit around the chest, and attach all moldings except for those on the ends of the top with glue and 1¼-in. finishing nails driven into pilot holes **(See FIGURE N)**. Since the lid top will expand and contract across its width with changes in humidity but the molding will not, a solid glue joint along the width of the lid

FIGURE N: Attach cherry molding strips around the lid top and above the joint where the lid meets the carcase. Nail the ends of the moldings on the short ends of the lid to allow for wood movement. Use no glue.

FIGURE O: Install lid support hardware so you can keep the lid secured in an open position.

top would inevitably fail. In this situation, ream nail holes slightly left and right and nail the molding in place. **(See FIGURE N)**. Use no glue. Cover all nail holes in the moldings with putty.

Finishing touches
Sand the entire chest with 120-grit, 150-grit, and 180-grit paper. You may wish to go as high as 220-grit. Apply an oil finish (See page 141). Attach additional hardware. We installed chest lid supports **(See FIGURE O)** and brass chest handles.

Cutting dovetail joints by hand

The hand-cut dovetail joint is perhaps the most famous, and intimidating, woodworking joint. As with any other woodworking skill, mastering them is mostly a matter of practice. But with these joints, visualization also helps. For many first-timers, the biggest hurdle to get past is simply studying the way dovetail joints fit together until they make sense.

Dovetail joints require a fair amount of planning and a good layout drawing. As you lay out the joint, keep a few basic principles in mind: The dovetail joint has two parts: the pin and the tail—always begin making dovetails by cutting the pins first. For joint strength and integrity, the joint should begin and end with a half-pin. The angle of the pin should not be steeper than 80° (a 1:6 ratio of slope to pin depth). The pin-and-tail spacing doesn't need to be exact: the tails can be up to three times as wide as the pins. In fact, the pin and tail sizes can even vary within a joint, which creates an interesting look that's unique to hand-cut dovetails.

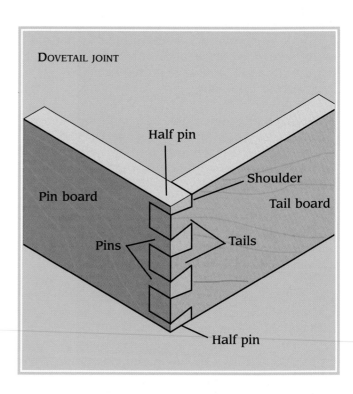

DOVETAIL JOINT

Half pin

Shoulder

Pin board

Tail board

Pins

Tails

Half pin

HOW TO MAKE HAND-CUT DOVETAIL JOINTS

1 Draw the dovetail pin angle and use it to set the angle on a sliding T-bevel that you can use to mark the pins on the ends of the pin boards. Make a scale drawing of a dovetail pin and use it to set a sliding T-bevel for marking the layout lines for the pins. A standard angle is 80°, which equals a 1:6 ratio of slope to pin depth.

2 After edge-gluing and cutting the workpieces to size, begin work by laying out the pins. Use the drawing labeled "Pin/tail layout" to lay out the pins on the end of the board with a pencil and the adjustable square. (See page 141 for an example of a dovetail drawing.)

OPTION: Use a flanged dovetail layout jig to mark the dovetail pins. These inexpensive little devices can be found in most woodworking stores and catalogs. They're easy to use and yield consistent results. The only real drawback to these jigs is that they're not adjustable, and dovetails aren't a one-size-fits-all joint.

3 Next, mark the pin length with a marking gauge. This line lets you know how deep to cut, so scribe it well.

4 Finally, transfer the lines drawn on the end of the board to both faces of the board with a try square or combination square. These lines are your guides to make sure your cuts are straight.

5 Use a tenon saw, also called a dovetail saw, to cut the shoulders of the pins. Split the lines with the saw, favoring the waste side. Cut down to the scribed lines, but do not cut below the lines or the kerf cut will show when the joint is assembled.

CONTINUED NEXT PAGE

Hand-cut dovetails

6 Score along the scribed baseline with a chisel to prevent tearout when you remove the waste around the pins. To ensure a straight scored line, clamp a block of wood next to the scribed line and use it as a chisel guide.

7 Carefully drive the chisel into the end-grain of the waste area between the pins so the waste wood will break off cleanly at the chisel cut along the baseline.

8 Remove waste in half the area, then flip the board over and continue removing waste from the other side. The beveled face of the chisel should face toward the ends of the dovetails, with the flat face contacting the guide board. When all the waste is removed, clean up the cuts carefully with a smoothing file.

9 Once the pins are cut, lay out the tails by laying the pin board on the face of the tail board and marking the pin profiles. Use a sharp pencil so the marks are true. Also use a marking gauge to scribe a line on the face of the board, establishing the bottom line for the tails. Make sure the pin board and tail board are flush at the edges before making any marks.

10 Draw straight cutting lines across the end of the tail board, using a combination square or try square. The cutting lines should align with the outline marks transcribed from the pin board.

11 Clamp the board in a vise and use a dovetail saw to make the cuts down to the scribed line. Remove the waste from between the tails with a sharp chisel, the same way you removed the waste from the pin boards. Make the shoulders of the tail board by sawing along the base line to the first tail on each end.

12 Prepare for glue-up by cutting wood cauls the width of the assembly and lining the cauls with masking tape. Apply glue to the pins and the inside edges of the tails, then assemble the joints. The joint should be tight enough that it must be tapped together with a mallet. Use a block of wood between the mallet and the workpiece to keep from damaging the joints or the workpiece. Offset the cauls from the dovetail joints and clamp them (offsetting allows the joint to close if it's cut slightly deep, so the ends of the pins protruding beyond the outer surfaces of the tailboard don't interfere with the clamp). Sand or file any long pins flush with the tail board where they can be sanded or filed down.

WOODWORKING SKILLS
Cutting finger joints with a jig

Finger joints (sometimes called *box joints*) typically are made on a table saw with a dado-blade set and a jig—an auxiliary board screwed or clamped to the miter gauge. When joining parts of equal thickness, a finger joint is a good choice because it's strong and effective. Like a dovetail, the finger joint is visible after it's assembled—a plus if you like to show off your handiwork (and what woodworker doesn't?). Unlike dovetail pins, finger joint pins are straight, so it's an easier joint to make than a dovetail, although it's not as strong.

To make accurate box joints, first rip-cut and cross-cut the parts to size. Cut some test slots in waste pieces with the dado blade set and check the fit of an actual workpiece in the slot. The workpiece should fit snugly without having to pound it in.

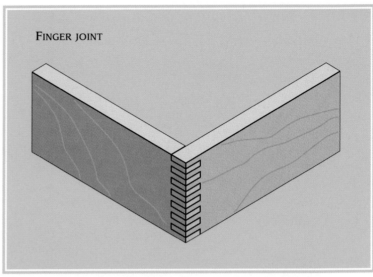

FINGER JOINT

Also known as box joints, finger joints are a good choice for joining two work-pieces that are the same thickness. The mating boards in the joint are identical, except that the notches are offset the thickness of one notch on one of the boards. A table saw with a jig can be used for cutting finger joints. You can also use a router (you can buy specialty finger-joint shapers) or a radial arm saw with the blade spinning on a horizontal plane.

HOW TO MAKE A FINGER JOINT ON THE TABLE SAW

1 Install a dado-blade set and throat plate in your table saw (See page 27). Set the cutting width of the dado-set to equal the thickness of the finger pins to be cut. Raise the blade set to cut the full depth of the pins. Clamp an auxiliary fence board to your table saw miter gauge. The board should be about 6 in. wide and at least 18 in. long. Make a pass of the auxiliary fence over the blade, then cut a strip of hardwood to use as a pin to fit in the slot, and glue it into the fence slot.

2 Reset the auxiliary fence by moving it a distance equal to the thickness of one pin to the outside edge of the blade set. Reclamp or screw the fence to the miter gauge.

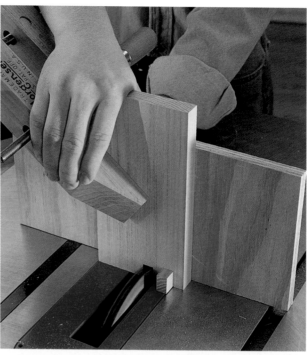

3 With the pin spacer inserted in the fence slot and the fence in position, butt the first workpiece against the strip and make the first pass. You can hold the workpiece in place by hand or clamp it to make the cut. After the workpiece and fence clear the blade, shut off the saw and back the workpiece off.

4 Reposition the workpiece by placing the slot you just cut over the pin space, then make the next cut. Continue in this manner until all the joints in that board are cut. Flip the board end-for-end and cut the fingers on the other end of the board the same way.

5 To cut the joints in the mating boards, fit the last notch you cut in the first piece over the pin, then butt the mating piece against the first piece, creating a one-notch offset. Make the first pass on the mating piece. Now remove the first piece, butt the notch in the mating piece against the pin and make the second pass. Continue until all the joints are cut in one end, then flip the board end-for-end and repeat.

6 When all the joints are cut, the pieces are ready for assembly. Glue the joints and clamp them together with wood cauls offset from the joints to allow the joints to close (See page 153).

WOODWORKING SKILLS
Attaching a lid with sliding-dovetail battens

Chest lids and tabletops are more subject to wood movement than just about any other furniture part. When attaching them to your woodworking project, you need to use a method that holds the lid or top securely in place, yet allows it to move slightly as the wood expands and contracts. There are special hardware clips and many other tricks for accomplishing this. One of the neatest and most effective ways is to use wood battens attached to the lid frame or table apron to attach the top panel.

To be effective, the battens need to be securely attached to the lid or apron frame. To avoid using screws, we cut sliding dovetail pins in the ends of the battens, then cut matching dovetail grooves in the inside faces of the frame. The stopped dovetail grooves in the front and back of the lid frame should be cut before you assemble the lid frame. To allow the top panel to move, cut slot-shaped guide holes for the screws into the battens (but the center screw in each batten should be driven into a standard counterbored pilot hole).

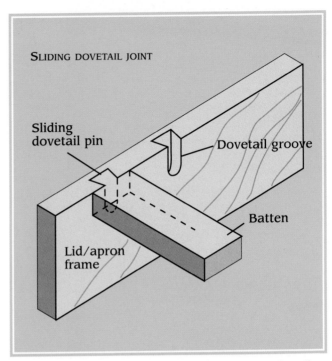

SLIDING DOVETAIL JOINT

Sliding dovetail pin

Dovetail groove

Lid/apron frame

Batten

A sliding dovetail pin on both ends of each batten fits into a dovetail groove cut into the inside of the lid or apron frame.

HOW TO MAKE A SLIDING DOVETAIL JOINT WITH A ROUTER

1 To make the dovetail grooves, lay out the batten locations on the frame parts according to your plan—generally, position a batten near each end, and space the inner battens evenly every 18 to 24 in. Install a dovetail bit in your router. Measure the distance between the edge of the router base and the center of the bit (called the router "setback"), then clamp a simple "L" jig over the workpiece. The jig should be square to the workpiece, and positioned so the bit will travel between the edges of the groove outline, stopping when the planned length of the groove is attained.

2 Set the bit to cut the groove to the desired depth, then cut the stopped dovetail grooves in the lid front and back. Using the jig as a router guide, make the dovetail grooves in the workpiece, then set up for the next groove. Make sure that grooves on opposing workpieces are aligned exactly.

3 Once the grooves are cut, assemble the lid frame (or apron frame, if making a table). Measure the length of the battens by adding the depth of the grooves to the inside dimension of the frame, then rip the battens to width and cut them to length. Also cut a test piece the same width as the batten.

4 Cut sliding dovetail pins on the batten ends on a router table with a jig (two pieces of wood joined at a right angle with an overlap on one member equal to the height of the router table fence). Install the same bit used to cut the grooves into your router. Trace the shape and location of the dovetail groove onto the end of the workpiece, then set the bit cutting depth to cut a matching pin (use test pieces until you get it right). Make the cuts in two passes and test-fit the pins in the grooves. Cut a pin on both ends of all battens. Be sure to clamp workpieces to the jig.

5 Bore screw guide holes in each batten. The holes should be large enough for the shank of the screw to fit in without friction. Slot the holes near the ends of the batten by boring two or three adjacent holes, then cleaning the waste from between the holes with a chisel. The slotted holes allow the screws to move as wood moves. Drill a standard counterbored pilot hole for a fixed screw in the center of each batten.

6 Dry-fit the battens to make sure they're flush with the top edge of the frame. The battens can be slightly below the frame. If they extend above the frame, plane the battens down, otherwise they'll prevent the top from laying flush on the frame. Glue the battens into the lid frame. Use clamps if necessary to keep the battens in place, flush with the top edge of the lid frame. After the glue sets, drive screws through the guide holes in the battens and into the lid top or table top.

Index